FEEL at HOME

FEEL
H(at)OME

Home Staging Secrets
for a Quick and Easy Sell

TORI TOTH

New York

FEEL at HOME
Home Staging Secrets for a Quick and Easy Sell

Published in New York, New York, by Morgan James Publishing. Morgan James and The Entrepreneurial Publisher are trademarks of Morgan James, LLC.
www.MorganJamesPublishing.com

The Morgan James Speakers Group can bring authors to your live event. For more information or to book an event visit The Morgan James Speakers Group at www.TheMorganJamesSpeakersGroup.com.

A free eBook edition is available with the purchase of this print book.

ISBN 978-1-63047-471-3 paperback
ISBN 978-1-63047-472-0 eBook
Library of Congress Control Number: 2014918495

Interior Design by:
Bonnie Bushman
bonnie@caboodlegraphics.com

CLEARLY PRINT YOUR NAME ABOVE IN UPPER CASE

Instructions to claim your free eBook edition:
1. Download the BitLit app for Android or iOS
2. Write your name in **UPPER CASE** on the line
3. Use the BitLit app to submit a photo
4. Download your eBook to any device

In an effort to support local communities and raise awareness and funds, Morgan James Publishing donates a percentage of all book sales for the life of each book to Habitat for Humanity Peninsula and Greater Williamsburg.

Get involved today, visit
www.MorganJamesBuilds.com

Habitat
for Humanity
Peninsula and
Greater Williamsburg
Building Partner

DEDICATION

For the man who stands by my side and allows me to follow my dreams, my husband, Sal Arena, love you poop!

CONTENTS

CONTENTS

Note to Reader

As a professional home staging expert, I've been blessed to work with some truly remarkable people and their amazing homes. Many of my stories are snapshots of my experiences with clients, and I've done my best to share examples that will help transform your own homes.

Also, please know I'm not a licensed real estate agent, builder, engineer, or architect and I don't claim to be. All such recommendations in this book should be considered as advice based on aesthetics only. For home pricing advice or home improvement estimates please seek out those professionals.

This e-book is for YOUR USE ONLY. Please be respectful. Unauthorized distribution constitutes theft of my intellectual property.

Additional copies may be obtained at http://www.toritoth.com

Foreword

APPEARANCE IS EVERYTHING!

I realize you might think that sounds a bit superficial and in most cases you'd probably be right. But in the world of luxury real estate sales it is one of the single most important things.

Having specialized in the Luxury markets in New York City for over 20 years I've seen just about everything. I've walked into homes that took your breath away because they were simply so beautiful and others that well.... made you hold your breath.

If there is one thing I have learned and that I try to get my clients to understand as we prepare to put their homes on the market is the importance of HOW IT LOOKS!

I'm the first to acknowledge that not everyone is a designer at heart and quite simply has the eye to understand how furniture, space, color and accessories come to together to make a room beautiful.

If you're not one of those people that's fine. No problem. We are all good at something. However, you need to either get someone who IS amazing in to do it, or if you're so inclined or working on a budget you can utilize the steps outlined in this book and accomplish remarkable results.

I first met Tori Toth several years ago through several very successful brokers in my office. I was looking for a great home stager to recommend to a client and they introduced me to Tori. I was immediately impressed with her presence, style and simple no nonsense, no drama approach to making homes beautiful. She took charge of the process with my clients and the results were phenomenal. It never ceases to amaze me how someone with real talent can totally transform a room.

Along with developing a long working relationship as my "go to" stager who successful helped me prep multi million dollar lofts down to studio apartments I have developed to have a tremendous amount of respect for her ability to take the ideas that come so naturally her, and teach and pass those ideas onto others.

She is a frequent speaker at national staging conventions and has over the years held many leadership roles in the different organizations that govern and promote the profession on a national level. Simply put she is one of the best in the business and recognized by here peers as a leader in the industry.

When she approached me recently about writing this forward I jumped at the chance. I thought the idea was brilliant and it was no surprise to me that Tori was working on such forward thinking project not to mention a daunting task. The idea of putting together a training system to help people develop the skills to make their homes more beautiful is in my opinion extremely valuable. Whether the goal is to maximize the value of their home when selling or improve the overall quality of life by being better able to create a beautiful living environment there is simply no one better working today to show them how to do it.

If you are thinking about selling, or just wanted to learn more about how to make your home more beautiful I highly recommend both this book and the training systems that are being offered by this stylish stager, Tori Toth!

—**Carl Ed Hardesty**
Licensed Associate Real Estate Broker
Douglas Elliman Real Estate
New York, NY
www.edhardesty.com

If you are thinking about selling, or just wanted to learn more about how to make your home more beautiful I highly recommend both this book and the training systems that are being offered by this stylish stager, Tori Toth!

—Carl Ed Hardesty
Licensed Associate Real Estate Broker
Douglas Elliman Real Estate
New York, NY
www.edhardesty.com

INTRODUCTION

By purchasing this e-book, you're one step closer to the closing table. Selling a home is no easy task. In a perfect world you wouldn't need to be living in your home while on the market. However, the list of reasons why someone sells is endless and in many cases forces a homeowner to stay put when selling.

The experience can be grueling for sellers when your personal lives become public displays to strangers and their criticisms. If you're going to be living in your home when selling you have to willingly be inconvenienced—not only emotionally, but physically. So what's the best way to get out from under the microscope? Sell fast.

Seems simple, but those of you who have been on the market already for months with no buyer leads can testify that many factors play a role in the final sale. The home has to be researched and priced right, you need a great marketing strategy, and your product (home) has to entice buyer demands.

Whether you're new to the selling process or your home is already listed on the market, it's never too late to prepare and showcase your home properly for sale. In this e-book you'll learn insider home staging secrets on how to make your space feel like home to potential buyers. When buyers feel at home, they're more comfortable and can relate to the space, which ultimately gets them to make an offer.

Make no mistake, the home sale preparation is more than just cleaning and decluttering. So if you're looking for results that end in the sale of your home, come discover how home staging can change habits and emotions that will benefit your bottom line—and ultimately put a "sold" sign on your property.

Chapter 1

BACKSTAGE
BENEFITS

S tarting off in the home staging industry back in 2009 while
training for my certification, I found myself skeptical that a home
could sell in days rather than months with the proper design
plans and renovations. Upon receiving my certification, I opened
Stylish Stagers Inc., a home staging company in the New York City
area, and sat back waiting for the phone to ring. A few days went by,
then weeks and months, and still I hadn't had a client who experienced
a quick sale, despite hearing about my competitors' constant success
stories: "This Long Island home sold in less than a week" or "My
homeowner's Manhattan penthouse was off the market in three days."

As I contemplated what I was doing wrong, I received a phone call
from a real estate agent to go look at her listing of a one-bedroom

apartment in Brooklyn that overlooked the historic Brooklyn Bridge. When I went to see the space, despite being fairly clean, I knew immediately it was a bachelor's pad complete with dated college decor, black smoky mirrors, and an uninspiring bedroom. The homeowner, a top MTV producer, had already been on the market for six months without one potential buyer. He gave me a tight budget to work with, so it was important to use what he already had while providing key accessories to enhance the space.

The living and dining room space of the one-bedroom Brooklyn apartment prior to staging with Stylish Stagers Inc.

Living and dining space after staging the Brooklyn apartment.

When I followed up with the client to schedule the staging, he said, "I fired my realtor, so staging isn't a top priority right now."

"Do you need another agent?" I asked.

The doubtful homeowner replied, "Yes, do you know someone?"

Well, of course home stagers know qualified real estate agents, and I put him in contact with a reputable Brooklyn realtor. The staging was scheduled the next day.

Stylish Stagers used his current belongings to update the space by accessorizing each room. We took a cue from his current artwork hanging above the dining room table—a Godfather poster signed by the movie's cast—and created a theme around that unique piece using other movie posters and pops of color to create a cohesive feel throughout the living and dining room space.

In two days we completed the staging projects proposed and the agent relisted the home on the market, this time with new photographs and a higher list price. Within seventy-two hours the agent called and said, "The house on Adams Street is under contract."

My jaw hit the floor. I couldn't believe my staging plan actually sparked buyer interest.

"By the way," the agent added, "he got above asking price."

I was so happy to have created a win-win situation for all parties involved. I was able to send some business to an agent, the seller was able to move on after trying to sell for half a year, and I got to stage the home and tell this amazing story that justifies *staging does work!*

After my success with the Brooklyn apartment, we staged more homes that had a quick turnover rate. Some homes sold in 24 hours, some sold within 7 days after staging. In 2011, Stylish Stagers staged 56 homes. Prior to staging, those 56 homes sat on the market an average of 231 days unsold. Those same homes, when staged, sold in an average of 77 days. That's 67 percent less time on the market! Oh, and as an added bonus, the sales prices on those 56 homes increased an average of 1-3 percent after staging.

Sell quickly and make more money—those are two very important benefits that outweigh the initial investment of home staging, but those are not the only benefits when preparing your home for sale. Let's take a deeper look into why so many sellers are turning to home staging before putting a "for sale" sign on their property.

Four Benefits of Home Staging

- **Move-In Ready Homes.** Today's buyers are looking for specific homes that won't require a ton of work before moving in. Hence, buyers want move-in ready spaces they can enjoy instantaneously. Home staging concepts show sellers how to prepare and showcase their homes with this statistic in mind:

63 percent of buyers are willing to pay more for move-in ready homes, according to a Maritz[1] consumer marketing survey on homebuyers. So why not get your home ready for its new owner?

- **Stand Out Among Your Competition.** While the market isn't as competitive as in years past, homeowners still find themselves up against neighboring homes on the market. How will you differentiate your home from those other homes for sale? One way is to stage your home, playing on emotional connection points that will appeal to buyers and stand out in their minds when it's time to make an offer. If two identical homes were for sale on the same block at the same price, but one homeowner staged their space to showcase the potential lifestyle you could have if you moved here, and the other home looked dirty, cluttered, and not well-maintained, which home would you buy?

- **Easier to Market.** Once a home is staged, the space will look like a cover spread in a home magazine, so why not take advantage of the light, spacious, well-designed space created and photograph each room with a wide-angle lens to market the home. Over 90 percent of homebuyers start their search online, and photos of newly staged homes will attract buyers not only to your photos but to your front door. Here's proof: How are you currently searching for your new home? Do photos determine your perception of the home? Would you go visit a home that had no pictures listed or had clutter center stage? Photos are just one way to easily market your home. With a staging plan in place, you will also have systems to keep your home looking like those online snapshots.

- **Increase Offers and Price.** Home staging often requires that some minor repairs be made to the space, which can prevent

---

1   Maritz Research Home Staging Poll 2005/2006.

buyers from low-balling offers because of the work involved to improve the home. Whenever a seller makes strategic repairs or updates to a home, they're adding value that could be tacked onto the sales price. A staged home creates more buyer interest, and with more interest comes more offers, so as a seller you could even find yourself in a bidding war.

Can you imagine making your goal to sell your home a reality that reaps these benefits? By reading this e-book you're now one step closer to the closing table, but maybe you're still not convinced staging will work for you. I'm here to make you a believer, like I became after staging and selling the Brooklyn apartment quickly above asking price.

Chapter 2

OVERCOMING A
SELLER'S OBJECTIONS

I could hear the sound of crickets. At times in my career, I'd send off a home staging proposal, follow up with the client a few days later by phone, then again by email, and then after a month, when I never got a response, I'd mark the project DEAD in large black letters on front of the file. The ratio between potential clients and paying clients began to shift when I discovered Zig Ziglar's book *5 Steps to Successful Selling.* In this groundbreaking book, Ziglar outlines the five classic "objections" that may keep a potential client from purchasing whatever you're selling. These objections apply no matter what product or service you're selling—including home staging. Ziglar breaks down all objections into these five categories that coincidentally many home sellers face:

- No Need
- No Money
- No Hurry
- No Desire
- No Trust

Now you're probably saying to yourself, *Tori, I know the importance of home staging; that's why I bought this e-book.* Well, I applaud you for taking control of selling your number one asset, your home. But you may still fall victim to these common objections as a seller when it comes time to set your home staging game plan in motion. So let's go through each one of these objections to overcome any setbacks you may face along the way when preparing your home for sale.

- **No Need.** As a home stager, I've gotten resistance from sellers about what needs to be staged in their home. Sometimes their beliefs are much different from reality. Despite my expert opinion, homeowners have told me they didn't feel the need to remove gym equipment from their living room or wallpaper from a bathroom. Many have thought their home already "showed" great, so they rejected the home staging game plan from the get-go. Others couldn't embrace the need to change their home, or they didn't grasp the overall impact of what a staged home could do for them.

Whatever the case may be, staging is a necessity in the real estate market. In fact, many buyers expect homes to be staged to showcase a lifestyle. It's imperative that you detach yourself from your home and its belongings. It is no longer your beloved home; it's a product that must be marketed and merchandised properly. So as you read through this book and learn the 10 Steps to FEEL AT HOME, have an open mind about what projects need to be completed around your home to maximize homebuyer appeal.

- **No Money.** This is a huge objection among sellers, and my answer to them is always "you have to spend money to make money." Home staging is an added cost, but it's also an added value—not only to your bottom line but to your marketing budget. So if redoing the kitchen, carpeting, painting, or bathroom fixtures seems like too high of an expense to sell your home, imagine what a buyer thinks when they walk into your home and see that all the updates they would need to complete before moving in have already been done. You can avoid low-ball offers or concessions from buyers by completing these updates prior to the sale and making repairs that will provide the biggest return on your investment and can actually increase the sales price.

Home staging is less expensive than a price reduction. According to a National Association of Realtors survey[2], homes that sold after four weeks on the market sold for 6 percent less than ones that sold within the first four weeks. So on a $500,000 home, that is a price reduction of $30,000. Home staging costs anywhere between 1 percent and 3 percent of the sales price depending on how much work is needed. That means on a $500,000 home, staging can cost anywhere from $5,000-$15,000. Which would you prefer to spend?

- **No Hurry.** You need to commit yourself to the process of selling your home from the beginning or you will just be

---

2   NAR Profile of Buyers and Sellers 2009, http://www.abor.com/news_media/ PublicAwareness/NARProfile.pdf

wasting everyone's time, including your own. If you're not serious about selling and just want to test the market, then home staging most likely won't work for you. The opportunity to sell your home is key during the first few weeks on the market. Serious sellers need to take advantage of this opportunity prior to listing and motivate themselves to maintain a staged home. I've had sellers inquire about staging, then sit on the market a few weeks and have an open house to get buyer feedback to see if staging is required before calling me back to say "I want to move forward with the staging plan." By then buyers have already seen your house and moved on to your competition.

- **No Desire.** Maybe you have no desire to pack up items, rearrange furniture, organize, or update a particular space. Maybe you question the process because of misinformation or lack of education. Or perhaps you simply don't want to be bothered.

Let me ask you a question: If I could give you the secrets to creating a fool-proof selling process, would you follow those steps? Would it be worth the trouble to you? I'm hoping you answered both questions with a yes.

In the following pages we'll explore *why* staging is such an important step to selling your home. That understanding will give you the *willpower* to stage your own home and maintain it while it's on the market. That newfound motivation, which comes from desire, will kick in when you want to give up because your kids have ransacked their rooms for the third time today, or you've busted out the vacuum for the fifth time this week. It's not easy staging and maintaining a home you're living in while on the market. It takes the right type of mindset, and that's what we will teach you.

- **No Trust.** Throughout this book you may ask yourself, *Why should I trust Tori? How does she know changing the paint color will work? What makes her the expert?* In the literary world, poet-philosopher Samuel Taylor Coleridge coined the phrase "the willing suspension of disbelief," which means that a reader gives the storyteller the benefit of the doubt—allowing them to carry the reader's imagination to outcomes they might not have expected. In the same manner, I will share my success stories with you and ask that you trust the process that has helped so many home sellers get the results they were looking for: to get their home sold quickly and for more money.

Trust the facts and statistics presented to you, but more importantly *experience* this process for yourself by putting yourself in the buyer's shoes. As a buyer, would you buy a home that needed an updated kitchen or bath? Would you be willing to paint over red walls? Can you imagine how much space is in your cluttered living room? By reversing the roles from seller to buyer, you may avoid seller's objections to home staging and receive a solid offer.

In the next chapter we'll explore what makes a home seller successful by zeroing in on six key mindsets that will set you up for success, or rather, a closed sale.

Chapter 3

INSIDE THE SELLER MINDSET

W hat makes a home seller successful? What does it take to succeed in the real estate market? These are not easy questions to answer, and I encourage you to think about them before putting your home on the market. What do you think it will take to start out and win?

To answer these questions, I've studied my clients and found that most success when selling a home comes from within the sellers themselves. It's about the psychology and practices of the seller, what is driving this person to sell their home, and what they are willing to live with—or in some cases live without—to get to the closing table. Within this seller's mindset you must also be realistic about the three key factors of home staging—*product preparation*, *marketing*, and *price*—that help close the deal. Without this framework, sellers lose focus, lose money, get frustrated and give up, or, worse, they never even begin.

Mindset #1: Begin with the end in mind

So where is the next place you will move to? For some this question may be scary to think about, for others the question brings excitement. Imagining what you want as if it already exists opens the door to letting it happen.

When you begin with the end in mind, you have a clear vision and direction of where you want to be. The steps to get to the end and accomplish your goal, in this case selling your home, become easier to navigate when you're able to envision your home sold. What do I mean by this?

Let's say you found out your neighbor just got an amazing price for his home, and you figure why not put your home on the market to see if a buyer is willing to pay for your house. You list with an agent and wait for potential offers, but weeks go by and no one is interested. As a seller you've neglected to prepare your home for sale, and the agent now wants to reduce your ridiculously high price to try to recoup their time spent and sell your home, but you refuse, explaining, "I want this price or I'm not selling." Sellers like this are most likely "testing the market." They have no real interest in selling their home; they're just trying to see if a fool would pay their price. They don't have an end in sight, only a wishy-washy attitude that will keep their home on the market longer than expected. In most cases like these, homeowners never end up selling.

Maybe you're a seller who has to sell because of a divorce, death, or financial troubles. When situations like this occur usually the homeowner doesn't want to leave their home, but they're forced out. Their goals don't align with the end results, so they may try to sabotage or stall the real estate transaction, unwilling to face the fact that they have to move.

Of course, you know you're at the end when a seller is sitting at the closing table handing over the keys, but a lot of factors go into getting to this point. If you don't make a conscious effort to visualize what you want, you can empower other people and their circumstances to shape this valuable transaction. To begin with the end in mind means to begin each day or task with a clear vision of your goal so you ultimately get to your destination: the closing table.

Mindset #2: Set feelings aside in a real estate transaction

Savvy sellers know that when selling their most prized possession, their home, they need to leave their emotions at the door. Owning a home is different from, let's say, owning a T-shirt. First off, it's a substantial investment that you own for years, in some cases the biggest purchase of your life, and it's where memories are made. Maybe the living room is where your child took their first steps. Or in the kitchen, you made your first romantic dinner. What about the backyard, where you used to grill every summer and have family reunions.

Just because you're saying goodbye to your home doesn't mean you're saying goodbye to your memories. Those memories will last a lifetime, not because the structure reminds you, but because they're valuable to you. Once a seller realizes that selling their home should be considered strictly business, it's easier to see the transaction through the eyes of a buyer. Asking someone to pay a fair price for a feature opposed to asking someone to pay a premium for something that's only valuable in your eyes will hurt your sale.

A couple recently called our company, Stylish Stagers, to discuss staging their home, but more importantly decluttering their belongings. They had lived in their Upper East Side home for over fifty years, raised three kids there, and were now ready to live the simple life in a two-bedroom condo. Over the phone, they mentioned removing items they no longer needed. The couple sounded excited to get started. However, upon arriving for the consultation, I got the cold shoulder. When I asked what they were interested in junking, the husband said, "Nothing until the home sells." Then he added that their kids or possibly future buyers might be interested in their worn-out belongings (which we know probably wasn't the case). The couple realized they had small items, like photos, that needed to be packed, but they couldn't fathom the idea of removing or rearranging furniture in their home. In their minds they believed the decades-old décor was just what buyers were looking for.

These weren't the first homeowners I'd come across that assumed buyers would like their home in its current state. We all have different paradigms or assumptions we use to make life decisions. Stephen R. Covey, author of *The 7 Habits of Highly Effective People*, writes that "we see the world not as it is, but as we are—or sometimes as we are conditioned to see it." Sellers are sometimes resistant to change their home's appearance while on the market because they use their past experiences, as the husband did in the story above. His thought process was "my home is perfect and I don't need you telling me otherwise."

Realtors face a similar thought process from their clients, although they're also expected to sell the home "as-is" for top dollar so the seller can move on. An impossible task if you ask me. "If [a seller] wants to make significant quantum changes [like moving], [they] need to work on their basic paradigms—the way they view themselves and the world around them," explains Covey.

So how can you obtain a cooperative seller's mindset?

The first step is to view the home as one of your most valuable assets. Whether the product you're marketing is beer, cars, widgets, or houses, packaging is a key component to every effective marketing plan. Property must be merchandized and marketed just like any other product. Think of a used car lot. When a salesman is getting ready to sell a used car, does he just park it on the lot with a price tag? No. The salesman gets the car detailed, writes up the car's features, and strategically prices and markets the car to lure buyers. It's the same thing when selling a home. You can't expect the buyer to see past your clutter and prized possessions.

The second step to obtaining a cooperative seller's mindset is to go around your home with buyer's eyes, meaning critique each room as a buyer would. Consumers' views have shifted as to what is acceptable in large part due to real estate and design TV shows. In the past buyers would seek out those fixer uppers, but today's buyers are willing to invest more in a home that is "move-in ready," which further supports the importance of staging the home first.

Home staging is not a fad; it's a trend. In a 2012 survey released by RIS Media[3], the researchers polled 600 Coldwell Banker agents and found that 45 percent of the agents said their clients were more willing to change the appearance of their homes to entice buyers this year over last; 94 percent of their clients said they would be willing to declutter, paint, and make minor repairs; 78 percent were willing to depersonalize; and 59 percent were willing to bring in new furnishings, artwork, or decorations to help sell the home. Are you following this trend?

As a seller, do not take negative comments about decor or curb appeal to heart. The buyer has never seen your home before and will have a much different opinion on the way the home is maintained. Rather than risk hurt feelings from buyers nitpicking over your home, I advise that you leave your home during showings prior to the buyers' arrival.

The final step to shift to a cooperative seller's paradigm is to get moving. Actions speak louder than words. When the couple above told me their kids might want their worn-out furniture, I replied, "Then ask them what they want and get it removed from the home." That not only began the decluttering process, but it put them in a mindset to start packing. I can't stress this enough. *Begin packing up or removing items you won't need prior to going on the market.* For many people, their home has been a cherished possession for a considerable amount of time.

---

3   RIS Media Coldwell Banker Agent Poll 2012, http://rismedia.com/2012-02-27/survey-reveals-sellers-more-willing-to-price-competitively

However, detaching yourself from the physical building emotionally will help make the transition easier to handle.

Mindset #3: Be proactive when showcasing your home

Becoming proactive early on in the selling process is a major turning point for homeowners. If you've read this e-book up until this point, I want to applaud you on being proactive because you've taken the time to learn how home staging can benefit your sale. Whether you know it or not, you're carefully designing an action plan that will get you one step closer to the closing table. You're taking responsibility for this deal and not allowing outside factors—such as the market's condition or your competitor's lot size—to affect your mindset.

Now that you're thinking about staging your home, let's take action! After living in a home for more than two years, it is almost impossible to "objectively" view the space from a buyer's perspective and thus spend your staging budget wisely. You no longer notice the elements of the home that may have annoyed you originally. This can be problematic when it comes time to sell, so recruit a home staging expert or a judgmental friend to go through your home and jot down anything that could turn buyers off.

A successful staging is the art of using marketing and decorating techniques to create an environment so that when buyers walk through your front door, they think: *If I buy this house, I can live like this.* This may include making necessary repairs to update the home, especially if the home hasn't been well maintained throughout the years. If you make updates on the home, make sure buyers are aware of the work completed.

Become proactive by putting a list together of what you have done to update your home, along with the month and year the items were completed. That page can then be part of a package that is handed to each person who tours the home. Inside the package, add some general information such as what time the mail comes, the name of the utility companies, and other information a buyer may find useful. Don't forget to include the average cost of your electric bill, gas bill, and water bill. These are things potential buyers may ask about when considering purchasing your home.

During the preparation stages for your home, I recommend following our 10 Steps to FEEL AT HOME process, which provides the steps all homeowners should complete before listing their home. I want to introduce you to the process now, but we will talk about it in further detail in a later chapter.

- Focus perceptions so your home stands out among the competition.
- Examine buyer's demographics and psychographics to l ure in potential offers.
- Erase clutter by using the "toss it, donate it, store it" method.
- Leverage home repairs for maximum return on your investment.
- Ambient lighting sets the mood to make each room more appealing.
- Tidy up your home so it looks well-maintained.
- Highlight positive features to showcase an aspiring lifestyle.
- Optimize space to enhance square footage.
- Modify decor by updating the look of your home.
- Exploit emotions to close the sale.

When it comes to maintaining a staged home, you can be proactive by following checklists and schedules and by dispersing chores to family members. It's important to keep clutter at a minimum, which you can do by removing items you don't use regularly and creating creative storage solutions to quickly hide clutter out of sight. A home on the market also needs to be kept clean and odor-free, which can be easily achieved if you clean up after yourself daily, rather than weekly or monthly. You're in competition with many other houses, as well as new-construction homes. Make your house feel as fresh as possible by thoroughly cleaning everything from light fixtures to baseboards.

There is one other way to be proactive when selling and that is by being a team player with your realtor to get your home sold. Make sure you keep in contact with your real estate agent by touching base, checking in, and finding out what's new. Ask them to report back to you every time they show the home. Find out if they've received any calls about your home. What are people saying about it? Do they think the price is too high? Get involved in the process, and communicate to the realtor your goals and end results.

Mindset #4: Control habits to reap the rewards

Individuals and habits are all different. Why do some people make their beds in the morning? Why do some people do the dishes right after dinner? Or why do some leave their bathrooms in disarray while getting ready in the morning? It all has to do with our habits, and since habits can differ from person to person, diagnosing and changing the patterns will also differ based on the person.

Now you may be asking yourself, "Tori, what do our habits have to do with staging our home?" They have everything to do with it! If you spend the time and money to stage your home, how do you plan on maintaining it? Spending most of my time on vacant staging jobs, it's always mind-boggling to step inside a home that has amazing potential but looks like a pigsty because of the homeowner's living habits. Dirty laundry piled high, dishes in the sink, dust bunnies the size of tumbleweeds rolling across the floor, surfaces that have never seen a cleaning cloth, and clutter buildup in every room can be a deal breaker when trying to sell a home. At that point buyers have a hard time seeing past the seller's unforgiving hygiene practices and move on to the next home. So it's up to the seller to recognize their habits and change their framework to make the home sellable.

In a perfect world sellers wouldn't need to be living in their homes while on the market. However, as stated earlier, the list of reasons why someone sells is endless and in many cases forces the homeowner to stay put when selling—putting their personal life on public display. So what's the best way to get out from under the microscope? Sell fast.

Well, that's easier said than done. One of the biggest problems a seller faces is dealing with clutter and cleanliness, especially if they have kids. When sellers hear those two "C" words, they tend to twitch and get defensive about their private space. If you have a home that's not well-maintained, it's important to understand why it is this way in order to help you move on.

It all comes back to your habits and the way you handle your household responsibilities. I'm always coming across homeowners who have excuse after excuse for why their home can't look like the cover of a magazine.

- "I don't have time to clean."
- "My kids are always dumping their toys on the floor, and I'm sick of picking them up."
- "I don't know how to replace the cracked tile."
- "Landscaping is too expensive."

The list of excuses is endless, but I'm here to say if you keep your goal and the end in mind, you can overcome these excuses and ultimately change your habits. Doing so will not only help during the sale of your home, but these will become lessons you can take with you to your new home.

Changing your habits won't always be easy, but if you acknowledge that you can reshape a habit, in time it will be effortless with this framework taught in *The Power of Habit: Why We Do What We Do in Life and Business* by Charles Duhigg. Duhigg says there are four steps to changing a habit.

1. Identify the routine.
2. Experiment with rewards.
3. Isolate the cue.
4. Have a plan.

Let's go deeper into each one of these steps. Duhigg mentions there is "a simple neurological loop at the core of every habit, a loop that consists of three parts: a cue, a routine, and a reward." In order to understand a habit you have to identify the components of a loop. Let's choose the habit of making your bed. This is a difficult task for many homeowners to complete daily. I myself have fallen victim to getting out of bed and not making it from time to time. It's a simple habit that takes a few minutes a day to complete, and it can have a powerful impact on your life, which we will discuss, but first let's dissect this habit.

In order to change this behavior and start making my bed daily, the habit loop needs to be determined. The first step is to identify the routine, which is the most obvious, the habit you want to change. So my routine is this: I get up in the morning, walk into the bathroom, put my contacts in, and start getting ready, then I go downstairs.

Once you've figured out the habit the next questions you need to ask are: What's the cue for this routine? Is it time? Is it because no one sees your bed? Not wanting to disturb your dogs? You hate mornings? You'll just be sleeping in it again later? And what's the reward? Being on time? Not disturbing the dogs? More sleep?

The second step to changing a habit loop is to experiment with the rewards. Rewards satisfy a craving, which drives our behavior. There is no particular timeframe on how long it will take to detect the reward. So take some time and determine all the rewards. For instance, on day one go to sleep earlier to see if you're more rested, on another day sleep in, on another get your animals off the bed when you get out of bed, and so on. The idea is to test different rewards to figure out what craving is driving your routine. Then write down how you feel each day when testing the rewards; you can even add a timer to help experiment what you're actually craving.

The third step is to isolate the cue, which can be a little more challenging. Duhigg writes, "Identify categories of behaviors ahead of time to scrutinize in order to see patterns." He goes on to say all habitual cues can fit into one of these categories: *location, time, emotional state, other people*, and *immediately preceding action*. So, in a journal, write down the answers to these five questions every time the urge to engage in the habit hits:

1. Where are you?
2. What time is it?
3. What's your emotional state?
4. Who else is around?
5. What action preceded the urge?

After a few days you should be able to see a pattern as to why you don't make the bed. For me, I didn't make the bed when I was alone. I figured out in step two that it wasn't laziness driving my behavior. The reward I was seeking was starting my day and getting downstairs. And the habit, I now knew, was triggered when I saw the dogs still in bed.

The final step, step four, is to have a plan. Once you've discovered your habit loop—the cue, routine, and reward—you change to a better routine by planning for the cue and choosing a behavior that delivers the reward you are craving, according to Duhigg. A habit is a choice we make at some point, then stop thinking about but still continue to do. In this step my plan was simple. Every time I got out of bed in the morning, I would get the dogs out of the bed too so I could make the bed before going downstairs. To make sure I remembered, I put a sticky note on the bedroom door that I would see before heading downstairs. There were some days I forgot to make the bed, but after two months, I lost the note and was still making my bed every day.

This habit reformation has prompted me to change other habits. Duhigg suggests making your bed every morning correlates with better productivity and stronger skills at sticking with a budget. It has also been suggested that making your bed boosts happiness. Now you may be thinking, *How does a task that only takes a few minutes a day change so much?* Duhigg describes making your bed as a keystone habit. Keystone habits are those routines that, if you can identify them, spill over to other habits. According to Duhigg, changing or cultivating keystone habits "helps other habits to flourish by creating new structures, and they establish cultures where change becomes contagious." A keystone habit is essentially a catalyst for other good habits.

After making my bed for two months straight, I found it easier to put away my clothes on a daily basis, do laundry on a regular basis, and keep the entire house tidier. On the days I didn't make my bed I often left clothes lying around my floor, dishes in the sink, and overall I felt unproductive. Don't believe me? Try it for yourself and see how changing a keystone habit can improve other areas of your life.

Mindset #5: Focus on the buyer's wants and needs

While I've asked you to focus on yourself as you prepare your home for sale, it's equally important to focus on the buyer's wants and needs. Have a clear vision of the end in mind and a focused mindset that revolves around the potential buyer and you will get offers. An effective communicator will first seek to understand another's point of view before seeking to be understood. In order to be an effective communicator when selling your home, you need to figure out who your potential buyer is. How old are they? Do they have kids? Are they travelers? By determining the buyer's demographics and psychographics, which we will explore further in chapter six, you can ultimately tailor your home to give buyers what you know they want, before they even do.

Now, you don't have to be a mind-reader, but if you take cues from your neighborhood and study those that live in the area (even on your block), you can usually determine what type of person will buy your home. When you review each room in your home based on what a particular buyer will want and need, you're subliminally marketing your home to lure the right buyers. Just like casting a net when you go fishing, realtors use a wide range of marketing techniques to attract the majority, but are they using the right bait to lure that perfect sale?

Chances are no. Open houses, website campaigns, and newspaper ads can be a waste of time and money in this economy if you're not targeting the right buyer. A home in an older community is going to attract a different buyer than a condo in the suburbs.

So many successful sellers research their markets not only to determine the buyer, but to find a real estate agent with a proven track record who can help get their home sold. While it's true that for each neighborhood the buyer's likes and dislikes may vary, there are a few things the majority of buyers are looking for.

According to a Maritz survey[4], more than 63 percent of homebuyers are willing to pay more for move-in ready homes. This means if you create move-in ready spaces that are updated and appealing, with all minor repairs completed, you will most likely

4   Maritz Research Home Staging Poll 2005/2006.

get an offer—and maybe even one that's more than expected. We also know that current buyers want more out of their home. They're looking for more positive features like built-ins, fireplaces, surround sound, green features, extra bedrooms, offices, and large family rooms. These buyers are family oriented, and they're willing to wait for a good deal to get what they want.

Today's buyers are smart. They can easily compare homes and shop around for the best deals thanks to the current technology. Successful sellers use this to their advantage: they research the competition. You can see what a neighboring home looks like, what it's selling for, how long it's been on the market, and then adjust your listing to look more appealing to potential buyers.

Since more than 90 percent of homeowners start their searches online, that means you need to have attractive photos to showcase to those online buyers and get them to your front door. Here are some tips to use when shooting photographs to market your space:

- Remove all clutter from the area you want to shoot.
- If possible, shoot with a wide-angle-lens camera.
- Have enough lighting; turn on all the lights so pictures look light and bright.
- When taking photos make sure to look in the viewfinder to see imperfections.
- Take photos from every corner in your room, as well as from up above and down below. Get all angles!
- Snap away; take lots of photos then delete the ones that don't look appealing online.
- Shoot with the flash on and off to have different lighting options.
- Use editing software like Photoshop or PicMonkey.com to enhance the photos.

Put as many photos of your home as you can online to show buyers you have nothing to hide. Make sure to review your listing online so that it stands out among your competition. Just because you have a realtor doesn't mean you can't suggest ways to improve the selling process. If you have an idea for an advertising approach, want photos that reflect the proper season, or don't like your home's ad wording, suggest changing it and be part of the process.

Mindset #6: Create win-win situations

Successful sellers know their effectiveness is largely achieved through a team effort. A win-win situation means making agreements or solutions that are mutually beneficial and satisfying to all parties involved. Let's go back to the win-win situation mentioned in the beginning of the book, where the MTV producer's Brooklyn home sold within seventy-two hours of staging it. The homeowner in this case possessed an abundance mentality, where he believed there was plenty for everyone and he trusted the process of staging and selling his home. This mindset created a win-win situation for the homeowner, the home stager, and the real estate agent.

Stylish Stagers recently came across a similar win-win situation with a homeowner in the West Village of Manhattan. The owner had been on the market for eight months without any buyer interest. She actually got so discouraged she began renting out the home. She decided to relist with another agent, who recommended home staging and increasing the price from $580,000 to $600,000. We staged the entire space quickly on a Thursday, focusing on the living room and bedroom by bringing in furniture and accessories that influenced the potential buyer's lifestyle.

That same day the photographer came with the real estate agent and took photos. The realtor then marketed the home for an upcoming open house happening that Sunday. By Monday he had multiple offers to share with his client, who chose to accept a higher offer at $645,000.

So, for less than $5,000, we got to stage the apartment, the realtor made a quick sale, and the seller was able to move on after eight months with more money in her pocket. Now if that's not a win-win situation, I don't know what is.

Here are the before-and-after pictures of the living room and bedroom at our client's West Village home. We changed out the couch and bed and added a few other key pieces to balance out each room.

The team created a win-win agreement by following these five elements (outlined in Stephen R. Covey's *The 7 Habits of Highly Effective People*):

- Desired Results: What does your final outcome look like? Focus on the what.
- Guidelines: What are the ground rules, the "shoulds" and "should nots"? How should each person operate?
- Resources: What is it going to take? What resources are available?

- Accountability: Who will do what when? Evaluate results and hold accountability meetings.
- Consequences: What happens when we are finished? Both good and bad.

Let's take each one of these five elements and determine when they occurred during the sale of the West Village apartment.

Desired Results – We all wanted to get the place sold quickly and for more money.

Guidelines – The seller agreed to pay a certain amount of money to the home stager to rent furniture and prepare the home for sale. The stager would make sure the home was clean and ready to go for the real estate agent to sell the space. The agent would then market the home to get a buyer.

Resources – The seller needed financial resources to pay for the staging. The stager needed furniture and accessories to showcase the space. We also needed a floor guy to remove the bedroom's red carpet and refinish the wood floors. The agent needed to get a photographer and use assistants to market the space quickly and lure in buyers for an open house.

Accountability – Once the staging agreement was signed, the stager was responsible to get the floors completed before scheduling the furniture delivery. On the day of delivery the stager needed to set up the space, and later that day the agent would come by to evaluate the results and take photos to market the home.

Consequences – Once the staging was finished the agent would have an open house where he would get buyer feedback and, if all went well, an offer. In this story, he got multiple offers by the next day, so the seller had options to get more money and complete the sale in a timely manner.

Stories like this happen often when the seller is open to negotiating and working with expert team members like a real estate agent and home stager. With such a winning team, the seller needs to put their trust in the selling process and trust that the stager will prepare the home for maximum appeal and the agent will have their best interest at heart when it comes to pricing.

It's important to price the home right the first time, and an expert agent will know the comparables in your area that your home is up against. According to a National Association of Realtors survey[5], the longer a home stays on the market, the further below list price it drops. Homes that sold in the first four weeks averaged 1 percent more than the list price; four to twelve weeks averaged 5 percent less; thirteen to twenty-four weeks averaged 6.4 percent less; and twenty-four-plus weeks averaged more than 10 percent less than list price.

Be part of the process and research the homes for sale in your area, and talk with your agent about introducing your home at a price that will encourage buyer traffic, rather than working against the agent. I've come across many sellers who have trouble setting feelings aside when it comes time to negotiate. If the buyer is trying to negotiate then it means they're interested in buying the home; all you have to do is come to a mutually agreeable price.

Being stubborn about pricing is not creating a win-win situation. Many times sellers are stuck on the price and are willing to "wait out the market" until the market catches up to their asking prices, but in some cases that never actually happens. Sellers should not take a counter offer as an insult. Instead, consider the price based on advice from the real estate agent. Holding out for a higher offer is not always the best tactic. If you've done your research and hired an expert realtor, you need to put your trust in that person. Listen to what they tell you about

---

5   NAR Profile of Buyers and Sellers 2009, http://www.abor.com/news_media/
     PublicAwareness/NARProfile.pdf

pricing. If you believe your home is worth $500,000 and your realtor feels the selling price should be $300,000, be willing to come to a win-win agreement.

By adopting the six mindsets of a successful home seller covered in this chapter, you'll be well on your way to achieving your goal of selling your home. In the upcoming chapters I will reveal how home sellers just like you changed their habits and emotions toward their home to prepare and showcase it for sale (and how they got the right price for it).

Chapter 4

STANDING OVATIONS

O vercoming your selling objections—and adopting new mindsets—can be challenging because home staging is a fairly new industry, and many people still don't understand how to utilize its benefits. Yes, I believe home staging is a benefit to anyone trying to sell their home for top dollar. It doesn't matter how much money your home is selling for; every home can be improved to create an emotional tie no buyer can resist.

Moving on from the Past

Walking up the front steps behind a realtor representing a $2 million home on the North Shore of Long Island, I noticed the landscape was manicured and the porch was welcoming—nothing major needed to be done in terms of curb appeal. But I knew something was turning buyers off if the agent dragged me here, and as soon as she opened the front door, there it was staring me in the face. The decor was lifeless. While it did represent the aesthetics of the home, the decor didn't show off the home's square footage. Dusty fake flowers scattered around indicated that this home, which once was loved, had been neglected for some time now, and in fact that was the reason behind selling the space. The homeowner had gone through a divorce, and his wife, who decorated the space, had moved out. His kids were grown and he didn't need the maintenance of a big home any longer.

Robert C., the homeowner of this property, knew it was time to move on. He had to let go of the past, however, in order to reach his goal of selling the home at that price point. The staging plan mentioned redoing the kitchen floor, adding a dual-sink vanity in the bathroom, boxing up belongings, and rearranging furnishings. At first, Robert was hesitant. He didn't want to change the floor his wife had picked out, then he didn't want to pack the Precious Moments figurines she had collected. Despite knowing that he had to stage the home to get it sold, we had a back-and-forth battle, but in the end I won, staged the space, and Robert couldn't have been happier.

"I can't believe the difference you made to my home in such a short period of time," he told me. "I needed to move, but I was stuck in the past. You got this home sold in four days, and now I can move on knowing I've made a profit."

Light and Bright

A client named Peter was trying to sell his parents' home in Bayside, Queens, and decided to see how staging could help with the selling process. Peter lived in Switzerland, so his real estate agent was the major contact person on this project. Peter wasn't attached to the home, but he didn't have much money to spend on the home improvements I suggested be made to attract buyers. The house needed to be painted, wallpaper removed in the kitchen and bathroom, and most importantly, his parents' items needed to be donated or junked. Since money was his prominent objection, I told Peter that as a home stager I would manage these home improvement jobs, and once completed I would add a few key pieces of furniture and accessories to provide each room's distinction, rather than fully furnish the first floor, which could costs thousands of dollars.

By focusing on the key elements that could show buyers this home's potential, we helped the real estate agent sell the home within two weeks. We transformed the home from cluttered, dark, and dingy to bright, clean, and charming. What a difference that makes to potential buyers!

Many of my clients at one point or another felt like you: they wanted to take matters into their own hands and expedite the sale of their home. The problem was they didn't know how to do it so they consulted a home staging expert that could point them in the right direction. However, once the expert told them what needed to be done, they naturally resisted for one reason or another until they were able to trust the process and see the results for themselves.

Chapter 5

LESSONS FROM A SUPERSTORM

I was sitting at the dining room table working on my laptop and sipping Veuve Clicquot as Sal, my boyfriend at the time, began cooking my favorite meal (tacos!) for dinner. The television was tuned to the Weather Channel; we were awaiting a big storm.

Earlier we had bought groceries, moved our cars to higher ground, filled sand bags, and removed our Halloween decorations and anything else that could be blown away. The local fire department went up and down the streets of Howard Beach that afternoon, urging us to leave. "If you stay we'll be taking you out in a body bag," they said. "Take our emergency number, and Godspeed."

It was a warning the entire block took lightly, and it became an afterthought as we prepared dinner. Sal and I planned to sleep downstairs with the animals in case any of the surrounding trees fell onto the roof. The plan backfired though around 7 p.m. when we heard frantic knocking on our screen door and our neighbor screaming, "You need to close your front door!" I looked down and he was already ankle-deep in water. I dropped a towel between the storm door and the front door and slammed it shut. I did the same with the back door after watching my backyard turn into a stream that was about to flood the top step of my stoop.

For a moment, I thought we'd be safe from the water now, but then the water began seeping in from the floor moldings and the furnace room. The first thing I took upstairs was a dining room chair, but by the time I ran back downstairs there was already a quarter inch pooling on the first floor of our home. "Coco, Sasha, go upstairs!" Sal told the dogs as I tried to grab both cats. Our one cat, Tigz, was scared and ran under my office chair instead. I followed her to my office; the rug was saturated in bay water. As I grabbed Tigz, I yelled, "Sal, grab the yearbooks, the hatboxes full of pictures, and our computers." I ran back upstairs, placed the cat down, and ran back downstairs to see what else we could save. By then, the water was up to our ankles and it was cold. I took another handful of items up, then came back down and stood on the steps as Sal handed me items we needed: food, water, flashlights, electronic devices.

As I ran back downstairs for the fourth time, I noticed smoke rising from the left side of the living room couch. The water at that point was up to the electrical sockets. I yelled at Sal, "Get out of there! You're going to electrocute yourself." The electrical panel was at the foot of the stairs. He ran and turned everything off, then sloshed over to the table in the dark, picked up a few more items and came upstairs. We were safe, but stranded on our second floor. Every few minutes we would run down the stairs, trying to count how much time it took until another step was underwater. By the fourth step, we realized the entire block was pitch-black.

A car alarm went off. We ran to the bedroom and saw a boat floating down our street. It slammed into our fence a few times before continuing down the street. The car alarm eventually died, but that noise was then replaced with glass shattering. The water knocked over furniture, breaking lamps, vases, and other collectibles. We remained huddled up in our guest bedroom until we heard a loud thud. We crept back down the stairs and determined the water had knocked over our refrigerator.

This was the longest night of our lives. We didn't know how high the water would rise or what would happen to our home, let alone us. By the next morning, when we walked downstairs the

This was our kitchen the morning after Superstorm Sandy, October 2012.

water had subsided from our home, but the mess took days to clean up and months to repair. The floodwater destroyed our entryway, living room, dining room, kitchen, and my office where I ran Stylish Stagers Inc. The devastation around us seemed endless. We spent weeks without electric, heat, or hot water. We spent our days cleaning, fighting with FEMA and the insurance company, and trying to determine how to rebuild the first floor of our home.

We wanted to build better, stronger, and utilize every square inch of our home, especially since we had to rip everything out down to the studs. But where do you start when your life has been turned upside down in a matter of minutes?

The Turning Point

There was no time to waste. If Sal and I didn't stay focused on our goal to rebuild the home, we knew it would never be completed, and quite frankly, camping out in our small bedroom with our four animals was becoming a hassle. It was a tireless cycle that never would have been broken if we didn't change our mindset. Rather than sit back and wait for others to help us or feel sorry for our situation, we made a goal and changed our habits to take action and meet that goal. While other neighbors were just starting to gut their homes, we were already living back on our first floor. The entire rebuild took about four months to complete, and we definitely faced obstacles along the way, but this experience taught me the exact process of what it takes to construct a home from the subfloor up, and it's a lesson I use on every staging our company completes.

Keep Your Eyes on the Goal

Whether you're rebuilding your home or staging it, the homeowner has to have a goal in mind. For us it was to have our first floor living space back, especially the kitchen. For you as a home seller, it may be getting a certain amount of money or having your home sold by the time school starts. Everyone's goal will be different, but it's important to have a goal and stay focused on achieving it. This is what will drive your habits and decisions even on the worst days during this process.

I think part of the reason we were so successful in rebuilding our home in a timely manner was because we didn't lose sight of our goal. It was hard to come to terms with the fact that we lost ten years of our lives in ten minutes—memories we will never be able to replace, like a trunk full of 9/11 memorabilia or photographs of our childhood. But Sal and I both knew that dwelling on this catastrophe wouldn't get us any closer to returning to normalcy. A part of us knew that when we walked down those stairs the morning after the storm, we were lucky to be alive and everything else was superficial.

My emotions might not have been so composed about the destruction if I didn't witness the storm's wrath firsthand. Staying in our home that night changed our lives forever, so it was easy to make a goal that would expedite the rebuild. Many people questioned why we didn't just sell the house or raze it to the ground, or they would ask why we added custom finishes on a floor that could flood again. We say, "This is our home. We want to feel at home again."

A lot of work went into making ourselves "feel at home" in our house once more. While it's effortless to put up sheet rock and create the four walls of a room, what is going to be the purpose of that room? How is it going to look and feel? The expression "feel at home" means to feel as if you belong, to feel as if you are home, to feel accepted. This is exactly what we want buyers to feel when they walk into your home for the first time, like this home belongs to them.

Above, our kitchen prior to Superstorm Sandy.
Left, our kitchen after renovations.

I realized that by going through this rebuild I could not only teach homeowners how to expedite repairs and remodels but show them how to create a stylish, comfortable living space that makes anyone who walks into that space feel accepted. This FEEL AT HOME process has helped hundreds of homeowners reach their goals to sell their homes. These homeowners have also spent on average 78 percent less time on the market and have a combined increase in sales of $980,000 after staging their homes with Stylish Stagers, Inc. This process has not only helped me rebuild my home, it has helped hundreds of people move on with their lives—and it could help you sell your home too.

Now it's time to dig even deeper and explore in detail my 10 Steps to FEEL AT HOME process. Are you ready? Let's get started!

Chapter 6

10 STEPS TO
FEEL AT HOME

N ow that you have the right psychology needed to sell your home, I'll show you what successful sellers do to prepare their homes for sale. What do they focus on? What do they consistently practice? Let's take a closer look.

In many ways, the preparation steps a seller must master have to do with how they spend their time. A seller must research, develop cleaning habits, and understand furniture and accessory arrangement, not to mention learn how to leverage the positive and negative features of the home. Although this seems obvious, most sellers skip the preparation steps and head straight to the marketplace. Unlike other industries, our community—which includes sellers, realtors, investors, and builders—has not fully embraced home staging, mostly because they have failed to see the value behind preparing your home for sale.

In the real estate industry, agents and homeowners take most preparation steps very seriously. Homeowners evaluate potential realtors based on common knowledge of the area, commission, and how much money the agent expects they will receive on the home. Real estate companies invest money to enhance agent skill-building opportunities and career paths.

However, when it comes to home staging, sellers are often reluctant to spend money to prepare their homes for sale. One reason this sad reality exists is because of the old mindset that says, "we've bought and sold homes before, and they never needed a home staging touch." This lie has left hundreds of thousands of dollars on the negotiating table, not to mention giving buyers control over your fate. If you want to control your destiny in selling your home, learn to master these ten preparation steps to make buyers FEEL AT HOME.

1. **F**ocus perceptions so your home stands out among the competition.
2. **E**xamine buyer's demographics and psychographics to lure potential offers.
3. **E**rase clutter by using the "toss it, donate it, store it" method.
4. **L**everage home repairs for maximum return on your investment.
5. **A**mbient lighting sets the mood to make each room more appealing.
6. **T**idy up your home so it looks well-maintained.
7. **H**ighlight positive features to showcase an aspiring lifestyle.
8. **O**ptimize space to enhance square footage.
9. **M**odify decor by updating the look of your home.
10. **E**xploit emotions to close the sale.

Step 1: Focus perceptions so your home stands out among the competition

Every home seller must become successful at creating first impressions. This step allows you to develop a good sense of what your audience wants, and what it takes to ensure that you stand out among your competition in the market. If you're not well positioned while on the market, it's going to be hard to get ahead. That's why it's important to focus on the buyer's perceptions. You want to make sure your home is attracting the right audience and that buyers remember your home when house hunting.

A real estate agent bases the sales price on what they see in the home, along with "comps" (comparables), but if your home is less than impressive when they come to tour the space and take photos, your home will be priced lower and marketed poorly. So make sure you've staged your property prior to contacting a real estate agent.

Think of your open house as if it's opening night for your favorite movie. The stars would be walking the red carpet, dressed to impress, promoting the movie and creating excitement and buzz—that's what staging does to your home when selling. You want to put your home in the best light possible so you can grab buyers' attention as soon as they walk through the door, and as they walk through the home, it reconfirms their emotions that they have to have this home. That feeling starts online, then at your front door, and continues into your entryway or the first room of the home they walk into.

Barbara Corcoran, a multimillion-dollar real estate mogul, recently sat down with the Real Estate Staging Association's CEO, Shell Brodnax, who asked her what changes she has seen in the last ten years. Barbara replied, "Before, people would ride by the house, have a peek at the front, and decide if they want to see it or not. Now everything is obvious inside the house; everybody shops online. Nine out of ten people start their search there, and without home staging people wouldn't even come to see the house. It used to be an extra; now it's essential. Why wouldn't someone stage their home if they want to get more money?"

Why is right! So let's get you started on changing the buyer's perception of your home. I always have my clients start with this simple exercise: go through the home with a buyer's eyes, which means examine each room as a buyer would. This helps you detach from the space and view your home as a product. I make them walk around the home with a pair of plastic glasses on and I say, "Tell me what you see." One seller that I worked with never noticed half the stuff she noticed after this exercise. The entryway pictured below, before staging, would send any buyer running out the door. Shoes were flung by the door, the dresser housed random paperwork and toys, the room had mismatched furniture, and it wasn't cohesive.

Before-and-after photos of entryway on Upper East Side, 2009.

See what a dramatic transformation home staging can make? I still wasn't excited about having this large bookcase by the door, but the homeowner refused to put it in storage and there wasn't another place for it in the apartment, so we made the bookcase work in the entry and it actually opened the space up and made it feel bigger.

Here is an example of a home Stylish Stagers staged on Long Island. When you walked into the home there was a long hallway before entering the living room, and they had a dated mirror hanging on the wall. We removed the mirror but didn't have the paint to match the rest of the wall, so we got creative and painted a rectangle on the wall to mask the problem area, while anchoring our new entryway decor. We also used peel-and-stick tile to resurface the floor.

Before.

After.

Which picture would impress you more if you were a buyer? Which photo would lure you into the home from online? When you walked through the front door, which picture would entice you to see what's down the hall? The choice seems obvious. The staged photos of this entryway helped sell this home in one week. Can you even imagine what the dollar value is of a buyer's first impression? Barbara Corcoran does.

Back in 2011, Barbara Corcoran was interviewed on the *Nate Berkus Show* where she stated that a home staging can add at least 5 to 7 percent to what the home is worth! So let's say on a $500,000 home you can increase the value with home staging by at least $25,000. That doesn't come close to the average cost of a home staging, which can be anywhere from 1 to 3 percent. Let's quickly do the math:

the staging on a $500,000 home is about $5,000, but by staging you plan to increase your value about $25,000, so you gain an extra $20,000 just by staging. Can you afford not to focus on your buyer's perceptions?

That's why this step is so important; it lays the groundwork for the other nine steps. Think of it this way. Chances are if you're selling your home, you may be simultaneously looking for a new home to buy. What's on your wish list? What happens if you see too much clutter or an unclean home? Use the same standards you use to search for a new home to sell your current space. As you work your way through your home using your buyer's eyes, make sure to pay attention to the following and take notes:

- It's all in the details. Is it cluttered or clean? Are there minor repairs needed? Updates?
- Review the six areas of a room: the four walls, the floor, and the ceiling. What do you see? Is it eye-appealing or outdated?
- Remember to feel. When you walk into each room, how do you feel? Is it a positive or a negative feeling? Light or dark? Comfortable or cold?
- What's the first thing you notice? Is it appealing or distracting?
- Check out the items in the space. Are they updated? Is there too much or not enough furniture? Are they in proportion to one another?
- Be a profiler. Can you tell who lives there? Are there religious artifacts? Too personalized? Too many hobbies on display? Make sure the home doesn't tell too much about the current seller's age, sex, tastes, or habits.
- Can you tell what the purpose of the room is? Does the room have the right balance?

Left Brain, Right Brain

A buyer's gut reaction never goes away, so make sure to critique each area of your home or recruit a judgmental friend who can help answer these questions. Once you've created a "to-do" list for each room, it's time to make a plan on how you want to portray each room. What will the cohesive style be throughout the home? Where will furniture and accessories be placed or removed? This will take some visual thinking, which can be difficult for some homeowners who are left-brain thinkers. Most of the population is more left-brain driven, using organizational and logical skills to conquer a task at hand. The right-brain thinkers, however, use their creative ability and function—particularly shape recognition—to assess the world. That's why some homeowners can visualize the potential of a space while others have a hard time figuring out how to arrange the furniture or what accessories go together.

Left-brain thinkers like to deal with words or numbers. They assess things in parts and are time bound, while right-brain thinkers deal with pictures; they assess things as a whole and in relation to one another and are time free. When thinking about first impressions and how you're going to transform your space for maximum buyer appeal, tap into your right-brain thinking to create a cohesiveness throughout the entire space. When you're selling, you can't just hang a picture on a wall because the wall is empty; the picture should be generic enough to appeal to all types of people. It has to match the color scheme and be in proportion to the rest of the items in the space.

If you're a left-brain thinker, I want to share with you the tools needed to tap into your creative side to make a difference in your home. Take one of the rooms you analyzed during the buyer's eyes exercise. Now go to that room and review your notes. Through the power of your own imagination, you can visualize your new room. Make a list of what typically goes into that room. Let's take an entryway, for example; there is usually a table, a table lamp, a mirror and/or artwork, a place to sit, and storage for shoes and coats.

Next, write down where each of those items would go in the room. Be as specific as possible. Where will the table go? Will the chair go next to the table or by the closet? Will the chair be on an angle? Try to capture the feeling you want the buyer to have when they walk through this room. Is the room light and bright? Warm and cozy? Involve as many emotions, feelings, and the five senses as possible. What will the room smell like? What is the first thing they'll see? Then go through what is already in that room and around your house. Can you reuse what you have to satisfy the items on the list? If you can, jot that in your notes. If you're going to need to rent or buy a piece, start a separate shopping list.

Stephen R. Covey (*The 7 Habits of Highly Effective People*) writes about tapping into the right brain daily to change a behavior. Staging your home and maintaining your home are two different things. You can't just stage your home and expect this singular experience to change the outcome of your selling process, especially if you're living in the home while on the market. You're going to need to maintain the space, and that requires using your "right brain power of visualization to write an affirmation that will help [you] become more congruent" with your goal of selling your home.

Covey explains how to use affirmations to visualize the perception you want to create. "A good affirmation has five basic ingredients: it's personal, it's positive, it's present tense, it's visual, and it's emotional." So a good affirmation for maintaining the entryway, for example, could be something like this: *It is deeply satisfying (emotional) when I (personal) put away (present tense) coats, shoes, and other belongings when I come home to keep a neat and tidy home (positive).* Then you can visualize the act of maintaining a clean home daily.

One last topic to discuss in this section about focusing perceptions is creating a lasting good first impression. Your home needs personality, consistency, and an energy that excites buyers. A small thing like how you greet a buyer at the door makes a significant difference in how they will respond to your home, so make sure your product is attention grabbing and helps buyers feel comfortable. Here are some tips to generate a favorable impression among buyers upon arriving at your home:

Curb Appeal
- Stay on top of your front landscaping; mow the lawn and trim bushes.
- Power wash the home and sidewalks.
- Add a welcome mat and potted plants around the doorway.
- Paint your door to update the look of your home, update the hardware.
- Place a wreath or arrangement on your door.
- Remove all toys, figurines from the front yard.
- Clean all windows.
- Update lighting and house numbers; make sure they match.
- Repair the roof and gutters and update exterior paint if peeling.

Entry
- Remove all the clutter; keep coats, shoes, and other items organized in closets and shelves. Remove any excess knickknacks or family photos.
- Touch up or repaint the entryway.
- Vacuum your floors daily. If it's carpeting, get it steam cleaned and remove shoes when walking on it.
- Make sure all light bulbs work with the same wattage and are on when showing.

- Eliminate odors. Remove unwanted odors and replace with vanilla, lemon, or something refreshing. I like citrus-cilantro from Pier 1 Imports.
- Open all your blinds and curtains.
- Furniture shouldn't be worn out or too big for the space. If you have too much furniture, place some in storage.
- Match the lifestyle. The more expensive your home is, the more expensive it needs to look.
- Add some final touches strategically around the entryway: a table lamp, decorative box, flowers, artwork, and a mirror are just some of the items that can create a statement in this room.

While everyone has their own style, a homeowner wants to present a simple, clean, and attractive home for the next owners. There's a fine line between what should stay and what should go because it all depends on the lifestyle you're trying to create and the desires of the buyers in your area, so let's learn how to tailor your home in this next section.

Step 2: Examine buyer's demographics and psychographics to lure in potential offers

People purchase products or services based on three reasons: to satisfy a basic need, to solve a problem, or to make themselves feel good.

Demographics have to do with the facts of the buyer, things that can be categorized and labeled from a statistical perspective. Age, race, gender, income, religion, schooling, and kind of work are all demographic information, as are memberships, how many credit cards they hold, what car they drive, where they live, the size of their house, whether they rent or own, and how many people are in the household. Demographic information consists of facts and nothing else.

Psychographics center on the buyer's feelings and are not quantifiable with numbers. They include such determinants as how the target buyer feels, what they want, what is important to them, and how they make purchasing decisions. We can determine a buyer's psychographics after establishing the demographics.

So how can you determine a target buyer? To start, do some research in your area. With the Internet, you can use real estate sites like Zillow, Redfin, or Trulia to determine your competitors and take a cue from the way they showcase their homes. In your notebook, research your area on these sites and look at the pictures to see what has sold and what hasn't. Is there a common theme in the photos of the homes that sold? What are the colors of the rooms? What is the style of the homes? Are the kitchens updated? Whatever your findings, write them down because they may provide clues on how to stage your own home.

While these real estate sites provide some information, they may not be able to tell you the demographics or psychographics of the buyers in your area. Don't worry. If you just Google the keywords "demographics for (your neighborhood)" on a few different sites, it should help you target your buyer.

Creating a Buyer Demographic Profile

First let's create the demographic profile of your buyer. To do so, you'll need to answer these questions in your notebook:

- Who is living in your neighborhood?
- How old are the homeowners in this area?
- Are there more men than women?
- Are they married?
- Do they have kids?
- Are there good schools?
- Is this a middle-class neighborhood?
- Is this an urban area or the suburbs?
- What is the highest level of education?

- What types of profession do people have?
- What is the culture of the neighborhood?
- What is the dominant religion and/or political view (conservative, liberal, etc.)?
- How do colors and the natural elements play a role in the area?
- Can you as a homeowner provide any clues?
- Why would someone need or want to buy a home in this area?

By determining one or two types of buyers who live in the neighborhood, you can then go into the space and create "stories," rather than neutralize the rooms to appeal to all demographics. You will learn how to create these "stories" in steps 9 and 10 of the FEEL AT HOME process.

Remember, the psychographic information determines how the target market feels, what they want, what's important to them, and how they go about their daily tasks—what sports, arts, food, and stores they prefer, among other things. This is where your people-watching skills come in handy. Check out the stores in your neighborhood. Which ones are always busy? Which ones are new? This will give you an idea of the direction the neighborhood is headed. You can also discover the type of industry they work in and whether they're an animal lover. Matthew Finlason from HGTV's *The Stagers* says, "Target stage a home by keeping a particular lifestyle in mind." By using Finlason's concept of "lifestyle merchandising"—a term he coined—Stylish Stagers has helped target buyers. Lifestyle merchandising is a combination of researching, identifying, and building a plan between the home, buyer, and the stager's aesthetics.

Why is this important? When a home seller shows a property focusing on the buyer's wants and needs, they not only solve the buyer's problems but they make them feel good inside, as if this home were made especially for them. You want buyers to feel at home so they're more open to making an offer. The more items you can cross off their buyer checklist, the greater opportunity you have to win them over.

A dining room turned into a kid's playroom. A second bedroom now housing an office. We've seen these types of rooms in our friends' homes, or perhaps in your own home. A room functioning as something completely different from how it was set up is fine for your living circumstances, but it can deter buyers from making an offer. That's why I want you to do this step before staging your home to make sure you know who the buyer is.

Entryway of one-bedroom apartment on Upper East Side, used as a makeshift child's room that didn't fit the buyer profile.

During one of my first stagings, I came across this problem. The homeowners, a couple, had a one-bedroom apartment on the Upper East Side of Manhattan. They needed more room. Their toddler-aged daughter was sleeping in a makeshift room in the entryway, and they'd just had a second baby who was sleeping in their room. Talk about cramped quarters.

Using the space as a child's bedroom, rather than an entryway, obviously didn't fit the buyer profile. Most likely, the buyer would be either a young single person or a couple. The space could even be used as a pied-à-terre, but it definitely was not ideal for a

The same room, after home staging, became extra storage for the kitchen, as well as an entryway.

growing family. So we removed the bedroom furniture and painted the space a warm beige. This room was off to the right of the front door and led to the kitchen, so we kept the furniture simple, reused their hutch as additional kitchen storage, and added a mirror they owned to bring in light—and to quickly see how you looked before walking out the door.

In real estate, maximizing the square footage of a space gets the most bang for your buck. That's where functionality comes in. When a home is on the market, a home stager can easily provide decluttering, rearranging, and/or adding furniture services to help increase the sale. However, it's important to create two, three, even four defined functions within one space.

To figure out how to maximize the function of a room, use target staging by honing in on a buyer's lifestyle. Let's say you have a home on the market with two bedrooms geared toward potential couples with a newborn, and one partner works from home. Based on the demographics, obviously an office has to be created, which could become the dual function in the living room. If you don't create an office area in the home for this buyer, the sale could be a bust because they may not think there is enough space in the home.

Within the function of your room, it's important to create spaces where a little girl can play tea party or a woman can sit down to finish her manuscript or a man can play cards with his friends. It's these everyday moments that can transform these functional spaces into the dreams of how buyers want to live. Multiple functions means adding more furniture and accessories to the overall staging price, but that price could be returned to the home seller tenfold when a buyer discovers how efficient these hidden spaces can be.

Once a home is target staged according to function, demographics, and psychographics, it's up to your real estate agent to use that same research to target market to those specific buyers. For instance, rather than cast a net for a new family by doing an open house, think outside the box. Where do young couples with babies hang out? Where do single women or baby boomers go? These simple questions can help hand over the keys to your home faster.

Step 3: Erase clutter by using the "toss it, donate it, store it" method

Once you've assessed your home and researched how to attract potential buyers, the next step in this FEEL AT HOME process is to roll up your sleeves and get to work! It's time to erase the clutter. Let me clarify what clutter is. Clutter is a collection of things lying around in an untidy mass. Check out the rooms in your home right now. Do you see any clutter lying around? Piled up magazines? Messy paperwork on a desk? Too many appliances on kitchen counters? Clutter comes in all different forms and it lingers in most homes, so if you see clutter haunting your rooms, start the packing process early by removing it from your house. Small knickknacks, collectibles, excess toys, and miscellaneous papers should all be removed before showing your house to buyers. By removing clutter you're instantly increasing the visual size of your rooms, which is the point here considering you're selling your house's square footage and not your stuff. The three main reasons to declutter are:

- Gain more square footage.
- Showcase positive features in your home.
- Buyers can visualize living in your home.

Since clutter may be different from room to room and house to house, I want to give you a better idea of what to declutter:

- Closets/Cabinets/Drawers
- Tabletops/Countertops
- Clothing/Shoes/Coats

- Paperwork/Mail
- Collections/Collectibles/Hobbies
- Books/Magazines
- Toys
- Excess Furniture
- Indoor Plants
- Tools
- Bathroom Supplies
- Kitchen Utensils
- Electronics
- Outdated Decor/Artwork/Photos
- Office Supplies
- Food Pantry/Fridge
- Shelves/Fireplace Mantel
- Room's Corners
- Religious Artifacts
- Linens/Towels
- Kid's Crafts/Handmade Items/Gifts
- Yard Equipment
- Empty Hamper/Laundry
- Pet Food/Supplies
- Sporting/Exercise Equipment
- Outbox (items not belonging to you)
- Shower
- Front Yard/Patio/Backyard
- Bar Area
- Basement/Garage

Now before you get overwhelmed and decide to ditch this staging project because of all the things adding up on your to-do list, I want you to start small. Take one room at a time. (I recommend starting with the entryway first, then moving on to the other main living areas before tackling the bedrooms, basement, garage, and outdoor spaces.) Clear one closet, one shelf, or one tabletop, creating solutions to your clutter buildup. If you set a goal of clearing just one room at a time, then accomplish it, you'll feel more successful and motivated to continue on your clutter-busting journey. Beating clutter requires building new habits, applying new organizational methods, and creating new household routines.

Schedule a time to declutter on your calendar based on how much time you have before going on the market. Try to schedule larger blocks of time, from two to four hours once or twice a week, for maximum decluttering efficiency. Scheduling decluttering sessions brings the goal out of the imaginary and into real life. Once it's on the calendar, then it's time to figure out what to do with the clutter. I recommend using the Pareto Principle, better known as the 80/20 rule, which states that whatever you're doing, approximately 80 percent of the benefit comes from 20 percent of the effort. In our case, we use 20 percent of our possessions 80 percent of the time, so why not get rid of the 80 percent? Here are three main solutions to getting rid of clutter:

Toss It. If you no longer need the item, it no longer fits, or you have no use for it then it's time to throw it out. But before you do, see if you can throw a junk swap party with friends (maybe they'll have something you need on your furniture/accessory list to stage your home). If a party isn't your thing, follow your local municipality laws to get rid of the garbage, or consider hiring a junk removal company like 1-800-Got-Junk to get rid of the items.

Donate It or Sell It. Have items you think someone else can benefit from? Try selling them at a yard sale, online at Craigslist, on eBay, or at a consignment shop. This way any extra cash you get can go to the staging plan and improving your home. If you don't have time to sell the items or don't think they're of great value, find a local charity and donate the items. Most nonprofit organizations will pick up items.

Store It. So let's say you want to keep the items but don't need to use them this season or while your home is on the market. Start packing those items away in cardboard boxes, and make sure to label them clearly for easy access. Store them neatly in a basement or garage. If you don't have space for the items packed, then get a storage container or use a company like PODS, which can drop a container at your home for you to pack then remove.

Once you've gone through the items in one room and placed them into piles to toss, donate/sell, or store, you will bag and box those items and remove them to their designated areas. The remaining items in the room will be items you need to organize. It's important to try and handle the items only once, according to David Allen's "Getting Things Done" system. Take the time to make a decision about an item in the present so you don't have to handle it again and again each time you decide to get organized. It curbs the tendency to put something aside "for now," which could lead to more clutter in the future.

Decluttering your home may be the hardest part of staging, but once you've rid the clutter, you're one step closer to the closing table. Just remember: take it one room at a time and determine how to handle each item immediately. Everything in your home should reflect the buyer's vision of the life they want.

Step 4: Leverage home repairs for maximum return on your investment

While decluttering takes time, repairs take money. In this step it's important to fix all minor repairs you saw around your home with the "buyer's eyes" exercise to avoid lingering on the market. You should have found at least five repairs to make. If you didn't, go back through your home and assess it again. I don't necessarily mean making large improvements to your home, such as ripping out your kitchen or bathroom, but rather manageable projects that were never completed. Do you have missing molding? Cracked tile? Walls that need painting? Holes in the wall? Leaky faucets? Wobbly stair rails? Repairs like these add up and can scare buyers away.

What do I mean by this? Would you go into a store and buy an item off the shelf if it was broken? If you said yes, wouldn't you also ask for a discount at the register? That's exactly what homebuyers will do—either walk away or provide a lowball offer. If you're willing to take the lower offer then feel free to skip this step, but know this: you'll be leaving money on the table, and in most cases you could have made even more money than your original asking price. Don't you want more money? I know I do. So before asking strangers to trade hundreds of thousands of their hard-earned dollars for your home, make all those repairs you neglected over the years. This way buyers won't insult you by asking you to lower the price or consider concessions.

Establishing a budget is an important decision. Make sure to take into consideration that some projects may impact the sales price greatly by having a bigger return on investment. When discussing home repairs with sellers, I advise them to look at the most recent HomeGain's survey, reporting on the top ten do-it-yourself (DIY) home improvements for sellers. In 2012, cleaning and decluttering came in as the number one project you can do to improve your home. The average cost of this project is about $402 with a returning value of $2,024 to the home's sale price. That's a 403 percent return on investment (ROI). Follow this survey when deciding on what repairs to tackle in your home.

HomeGain 2012 Top 10 D-I-Y Home Improvements For Sellers (NATIONAL)

D-I-Y Home Improvements	Cost	Benefit	ROI	% Recommended
Clean & de-clutter	$402	$2,024	403%	99%
Lighten & brighten	$424	$1,690	299%	96%
Electrical & plumbing	$807	$3,175	293%	93%
Landscaping	$564	$1,777	215%	97%
Staging	$724	$2,144	196%	76%
Carpet	$671	$1,746	160%	99%
Floors	$902	$1,892	110%	93%
Paint Interior	$967	$2,001	107%	94%
Kitchen & bathroom	$1,957	$3,254	66%	70%
Paint exterior	$1,406	$2,176	55%	79%

© 2012 HomeGain.com, Inc.

www.homegain.com/sellertools   HomeGain.

Since all homes have different needs, here is a list to help clarify what each of these ten HomeGain projects means:

Clean and Declutter. Remove any personal items, remove clutter from all areas, organize closets, clean all areas inside and outside of home, eliminate odors.

Lighten and Brighten. This has to do not only with the light fixtures, but the light coming inside your home. Clean windows, doors, and skylights inside and outside, replace or remove curtains, remove other obstacles from windows blocking light, repair or replace lighting fixtures and bulbs, make sure windows open easily.

Electrical and Plumbing. Doorbell, switches, and fixtures should all work properly. Replace old outlets and all switch plates. Update electrical panels and consider adding new technology for appliances, Internet, and other equipment. Fix leaky faucets, clogs, and handles in sinks. Toilets should work properly.

Landscaping. Fix both the front and back yards by adding mulch and removing leaves, branches, and debris; plant bushes, flowers, and add planters around the front door and walkway. Mow grass, weed, and make sure to constantly water everything.

Home Staging. This means to reduce clutter and personal items and rearrange furniture and decor to show maximum square footage. Add fresh flowers, artwork, and updated decor.

Carpets. Steam-clean or replace worn carpet, eliminate creaks in floors, and make sure carpet is secure and not bunching.

Floors. Patch, repair, or replace hardwood floors and tiles. Re-grout or clean grout between tile floors, eliminate creaks in floors. Make sure pet stains are taken care of.

Paint Interior. Remove wallpaper, fix holes in walls. Add fresh coat of paint. Consider whitewashing dark paneling and painting front door. Get rid of all stains and watermarks.

Kitchen and Bathroom. Update appliances, repair damaged countertops, drawers, and cabinets. Update cabinet hardware. Update bathroom fixtures; sinks and toilets should function properly. Repair vanity, shelving, and towel racks. Add new towels and mats. Replace or update mirror. Replace or clean shower doors and shower curtains. Re-grout or replace tile where needed.

Paint Exterior. Add a fresh coat of paint around exterior of home by painting shutters, window ledges, front door, and garage. Also paint or restain fence if needed.

Other Improvements:

- Cracks in Foundation/Sidewalk
- Sagging or Broken Screens
- Restain Deck
- Smoke Detector/Burglar Alarm Work
- Remove Mildew (Outside and Inside)
- Replace Broken Blinds
- Fix Roof Shingles
- Clear and Caulk Gutters
- Eliminate Pet/Smoking Odors
- Reseal Toilets
- Update Heat Baseboards/Units
- Working Fireplace/Chimney
- Clean Air/Heating System
- Garage Door

By making these simple changes, you're adding value to your home, not to mention gaining buyer confidence. Completed projects will give buyers a well-maintained image of your house. When sellers don't take care of their home's cosmetic updates, they usually completely disregard bigger updates and maintenance, such as the heating system or the roof. Most buyers would think, *If this is how the home looks now, what is underneath the surface that I can't see?*

As a seller it's important to take a proactive approach in completing this step. Address any of the issues on the HomeGain survey, and visit www.homegain.com/sellertools to get a customized report on improving your home based on your zip code. All you have to do is enter your zip code and answer a few questions about the current state of your home, and this link will provide you with a detailed report on what improvements to make in your area as well as an estimate on how much it will cost. Genius right?

Getting a Pre-sale Home Inspection

Obtaining a pre-sale inspection from a home inspector is another way to address any issues with your home prior to going on the market, and I think it's highly worth the investment. For over twenty-five years now, homes on the market must undergo a buyer home inspection prior to closing, and in many cases this report can make or break a deal if an inspector finds something wrong with the home. Why wait until after you've made repairs, staged your home, and accepted an offer to then get a home inspection? If the inspector finds a crack in your foundation or mold in your home, your dream deal could become a dead deal.

A professional home inspector will examine everything from the foundation to the roof, looking for safety issues or defects that could become a significant issue for the buyer. To find a home inspector in your area, go to the American Society of Home Inspectors website at www.ashi.org/find or the National Association of Home Inspectors website at www.nahi.org. Be proactive; put your best foot forward and know your house is worth the price you want for it.

Making Major Improvements

The last thing I want to talk about in this step is making serious transformations when your home is in disrepair or just doesn't size up to other homes on the market. Major improvements—such as replacing the roof, kitchen, or bathroom—can be costly and in some cases aren't worth the money invested, but depending on your area, your home may need it to compete in the marketplace.

Buyers start by focusing on an area and price range. As they go through the neighborhood looking at homes on the market, they compare each home to the others and their wish list. It's like the HGTV show *House Hunters*, where the buyer tours homes in their target market, discusses the pros and cons, then ultimately chooses the one that fits their wants and needs. Buyer wish lists usually include some or all of these:

- Desired Square Footage
- Newer Home/Repairs and Upgrades
- Number of Bedrooms
- Number of Bathrooms
- Family Room/Finished Basement
- Fireplace
- Formal Dining Room
- Gas/Heat
- Central Air
- Eat-in Kitchen
- Tub and Separate Shower
- Den/Office
- Hardwood Floors
- Disposal/Dishwasher
- Laundry Room
- Newer Roof

- Landscape Sprinklers
- Swimming Pool
- Close to Schools
- Porch/Deck

This is where researching your market's competition can come in handy. In your price range, make sure you know which homes are on the market around you, which homes have recently sold, and which ones have been lingering on the market. Then see how your home compares to their amenities. If your home lacks what's on the market and on the buyer's wish list, you may fall short of a sale. So consider making these major improvements to win over buyers.

So what exactly should you improve when redoing the kitchen or bathroom? A seller should make sure they're adding value with all-wood cabinets, commercial-looking appliances, natural wood or stone floors and countertops. How many bathrooms do you have in your home? If there's only one, consider adding a second bathroom before remodeling with an expensive budget. Put it this way: if you've got a four-bedroom, one-bath home, it's certainly going to pay to add a second bathroom.

Every homeowner's first priority should be keeping the existing structure sound, so if you do a pre-inspection and discover the roof needs to be changed, you should spend your money there first before making cosmetic or luxury improvements. Another place to consider spending money is on the curb appeal of the home. If you update the inside of the home but the exterior still doesn't show well, buyers may hesitate and your home will linger on the market. Consider adding creative interest to the front of your home through adding a porch, overhang, or shutters, especially if you have a flat house.

Adding rooms can also be a good investment, particularly if you live in a hot housing market. In some areas, this demand is driven by homeowners who want more space but then realize they can't afford larger homes in their own neighborhood. According to a National Association of Realtors survey[6], they found that every 1,000 square feet added to a home boosts the sale price by more than 30 percent. Bathroom additions return the most value, with an average of 86.4 percent based on findings from a *Remodeling* magazine report. Adding attic bedrooms, family rooms, and sunrooms has between a 70 to 80 percent ROI, and that's because more buyers are looking for homes with unique spaces like a home office, craft, or exercise room.

Remember, you need to spend money to make money, and leveraging home repairs whether small or big can add value to your home if done correctly. Make sure to research your market, and don't add on so much that you price your house right out of the neighborhood. It's also important to know when to bring in a professional, not only as a safety precaution but to make sure the job is done correctly. Need help completing home improvements? Visit www.angieslist.com or www.homeadvisor.com to find qualified professionals in your area. When hiring a professional, make sure to research the company, ask to see their work, and talk to past customers.

Step 5: Ambient lighting sets the mood to make each room more appealing

When your home is on the market, it's all about creating a light and bright feel throughout the space to welcome buyers. A home seller can do this a number of ways by utilizing natural light, painting, and adding more indoor lighting. The more light bouncing around each room, the bigger the home will appear, and since buyers are purchasing square footage make sure you're showcasing the illusion of maximum space.

Let's first talk about how to enhance the natural light coming into your home. Natural light can provide several benefits in showcasing your home, while saving money in your wallet. Sunlight rather than

---

6   2005 National Association of Realtors Survey

light from a fixture can save on energy costs and boost a buyer's mood when walking through the home. Start by assessing the natural light in each room of your home. Does the room feel dark or light? How many windows do you have? How many doors? Would it make sense to update either of these or add skylights? Here are a few tips on how to intensify your natural light source:

Bushes and Trees. Overgrown trees, bushes, or shrubs in your yard can immediately put a dark cloud over your home. Trim hedges and prune branches away from the windows so your home gets ample sunlight. Also, make sure to clear the exterior and interior windowsills for optimal sunlight.

Window Treatments. Some window treatments can actually block sunlight from entering the home, like Roman shades, which are usually made of fabric that lies directly over the window. Heavy fabrics like velvet or tweed and dark colors can also weigh a room down. The best type of window treatment to use is a sheer light cotton or linen curtain that can hang on either side of the window. Make sure to have the curtains open during every showing. When hanging panel curtains, install the rod up by the ceiling so the window looks longer than it is, and be sure the panels flank the sides of the window; this way the window looks wider. Like this:

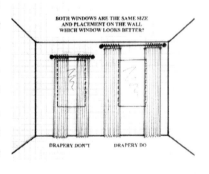

Replace Solid Doors. Solid exterior doors can definitely suck the life out of entries and exits. Try replacing the solid door for one that has a window. It will instantly add light to the entryway. You can also add a screen door so you can leave the front door open during showings, providing the illusion that there is more light in the entryway than there really is.

Add Natural Light Sources. Consider adding a window, skylight, door, or sliding door in a particular room that lacks natural light. The more windows and doors you have in a room, the brighter it will be. Before adding any of these, though, make sure to monitor how the sunlight reflects in the room. Do you get morning light? Afternoon light? As we were rebuilding the first floor of our home after Superstorm Sandy, I wanted to add more natural light in the home. We also wanted to add a door to the left side of our backyard. While this room housed our front door and three windows, it only received morning sunlight, so whenever we wanted to enjoy the room in the afternoon it was already darker than the rest of the home. We ended up removing the third window to replace it with a sliding glass door. Now this room is well-lit all day long.

Entryway of our home after Superstorm Sandy hit, October 2012.

Our entryway after remodeling. We added a sliding glass door where there used to be a window and a hutch.

Using a Mirror. Mirrors are a great way to reflect light throughout a room. Adding a mirror on a wall opposite to a window doubles the light streaming in and can make the space appear brighter. You can use a large mirror, a grouping of mirrors, or mirrored furniture and accents to bounce the light around.

Another way to make a room look lighter and brighter is by using the right paint colors. Dark colors absorb light while light colors and whites reflect natural light, so make sure to lighten up your color palette before putting your home on the market. You want to choose the color of your walls carefully by determining what direction the room is facing. Is it facing north or south? Does it get morning or afternoon light? How much natural light is there? For example, if the room faces north, avoid cool colors with blue undertones. Instead, opt for colors that are warmer on the color wheel and have yellow undertones. Regardless of the location of the room, consider soft neutral colors for your walls to appeal to buyers. Avoid stark whites and bold colors that could disrupt the buying process. Here are a few of my favorite color choices from Benjamin Moore:

Eternity AF-695	Shaker Beige AC-36
Palladian Blue HC-144	Manchester Tan HC-81
Revere Pewter HC-172	Bennington Grey HC-82
Sandy Hook HC-108	Abalone 2108-60
Shale 861	Smoke Embers 1466
Coastal Fog AC-1	Thunder AF-685
Pearl River 871	Silver Fox 2108-50
Castleton Mist HC-1	Stone Harbor 2111-50

Remember, wall color sets the atmosphere in a room. Use neutral earth-tone colors rather than all white as your wall color. You can choose a darker color for an accent wall. Dark molding and trim can absorb light so consider a lighter hue for those. When choosing a color for your room, take a cue from the items in the room such as the flooring, woodwork, tile, or cabinets. Paint finishes can vary depending on the condition of the walls and what rooms you're painting. I would consult with a paint professional when you purchase the paint. Also, go to www.benjaminmoore.com to learn more about the colors above and for other color combinations.

It's equally important to remember to paint that fifth wall, your ceiling. Over time a ceiling can look dull from dust, pollen, aging paint, nicotine, and cooking oils in the air. I recommend using paint sold as "ceiling white paint" because it is especially designed to be reflective. It's a pure bright white.

The final way I want to talk about creating a light and bright feel in your home is through indoor lighting. While this seems obvious, most homeowners have ample lighting in their home; they just neglect to change the light bulbs in their light fixtures once they've blown out. So take a moment to check your lighting. Make sure you have the appropriate wattage (use maximum wattage), and on a multi-bulb fixture be sure all light bulbs match.

A recent trend is switching out regular light bulbs for Edison filament bulbs. These bulbs can add drama, they're great to enhance industrial décor, and they provide an interesting artistic piece to the room. Also take note that if your fixtures and lamps are outdated or builder-grade, you'll want to replace them. Here are a few examples of fixtures that need to be changed. If you have them, please update them:

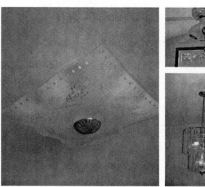

Remove lighting like this; it looks cheap and dates the space.

There are different ways to utilize indoor lighting. Light can come from ceiling fixtures, fans, chandeliers, table lamps, and floor lamps.

Even up lights or down lights (spotlights) can make an impact. Let's go over these different types of lighting sources:

Ceiling Fixtures. Overhead lighting is a must! Many homes in the New York City area have no overhead fixtures in some of the most important areas of the home, such as the entryway, living room, and bedrooms. If you're faced with this problem, the first thing to decide is do you have money in the budget to add lighting. Add a fixture in the middle of the room, or add hi-hat lighting so you have ample lighting throughout the space.

Ceiling Fans. Fans are a great way to circulate air throughout your home. However, I despise ceiling fans in the kitchen. Most homeowners don't clean their fans as often as they should, so when they turn them on dust from the blades can contaminate food. Use fans with a lighting kit, but try to avoid fans with control chains. Get fans with remote controls instead. Also, pay attention to the fans' finishes and that they match the finishes throughout the room. Add ceiling fans in bedrooms, living rooms, and great rooms.

Chandeliers/Pendant Lighting. This type of lighting is a great way to add bling to a room. Chandeliers are a statement piece, so be sure to choose one that matches the home's aesthetic and style decor. I recommend using a chandelier in an entryway, dining room, or master bedroom. Add something big, bold, and reflective. A pendant light is ideal over kitchen islands. Hang pendant lights approximately thirty to thirty-six inches above your countertops.

Table Lamps. A table lamp is a great way to update a space; it's budget friendly and can add a huge impact on the overall feel of the home. Table lamps come in different sizes, colors, and shapes. Choose lamps that match the home's decor and are proportionate to the other items in the room. Swap your shade by using neutral, patterned, or textured lampshades. Find shades at www.target.com. They have a vast variety and are inexpensive. A drum shade can instantly update a lamp. Be sure to avoid dark lampshades that absorb light. In order to be effective a lamp needs to be turned on. Don't rely on your realtor to turn on all the lights when showing a home; put lamps on timers to make sure dark rooms are always well-lit.

Floor Lamps. Like table lamps, floor lamps are great to add extra light in a space where a table won't necessarily fit. Put a floor lamp next to a couch or chair. Be strategic about placement though. Try to make cords invisible, rather than having an extension cord out for buyers to trip on. Also, look for a lamp that provides ample light and doesn't take up a lot of square footage.

Up Lights/Down Lights (Spotlights). This type of light is a perfect way to highlight positive features in the room and add some drama. Add an up light in a dark corner behind a piece of furniture or plant to instantly create a spacious look and make your room glow. Add to artwork, fireplaces, dark corners, and built-ins.

Once you've chosen what type of lighting will be in the room, the next step is to strategically place lighting throughout the room so it's equally lit to maximize the space. This technique is known as the triangular effect, where you use at least three sources of light to essentially create a triangle on the design sketch. Here's an example:

With the triangular effect, you can use multipurpose fixtures; you can create ambience with overhead lighting and two other light sources, such as table lamps. Remember, the more light sources you have in a room the more spacious it will appear to buyers.

When it comes time to show your home, encourage your real estate agent to show the space

See how the lamps create a triangle? This shows that you have ample lighting in the room.

when it looks best. For example, if your kitchen gets morning sun, but during that time your bedrooms are dark, then it's a perfect time to show your home in the morning because buyers won't mind the dark bedrooms. Or let's say you have an amazing sunset view over the water every evening—that's when you want to show the home. Also, whenever possible, try to avoid showing your home on dark and rainy days.

Step 6: Tidy up your home so it looks well-maintained

After the belongings have been reused or removed, it's time to clean the house like it's never been cleaned before. Right now, make a commitment: either you and your family will be held responsible for keeping your home clean, or you'll need to hire a cleaning service. Either way, the more you do to keep your home clean the easier it will be to sell, so take a few minutes to put a plan in place. What cleaning tasks need to be completed? Who is responsible for what tasks? What are the rewards for completing the task? What are the consequences? How many times a week does a task need to be completed? Answer these questions and/or research cleaning companies to determine how your home will remain spic and span while on the market.

All homes must be cleaned prior to showings and open houses, so sellers must be responsible for daily cleaning touch-ups like dirty dishes and laundry. The key to keeping a tidy home is to clean up as you go throughout your daily activities.

Let's take cooking dinner, for example. Do you use every pot, pan, and dish to cook? Do you leave food and spices out on the countertop after using them in your recipe? How do you handle spills on the countertop or floor while cooking? If you don't clean up throughout the cooking process, you'll have a big mess to deal with after you've stuffed your face, and who wants to clean then? I know not me. In my house we rinse cookware and put it in the dishwasher after using it. We take a few more steps and put food back in the fridge rather than leave it out, and if something spills we take a minute to wipe it up. This way when we're finished eating the only things we have left to clean are our plates and a few pots.

It's also important to designate a few chores a day to complete. This way you won't feel overwhelmed, which can deter you from cleaning at all. Create a schedule, take one room at a time (sound familiar?), and begin cleaning.

There is a method to the cleaning madness, and if you could take away one tip to help clean your home this is it: *clean from the top down.* What do I mean by this? Start from the ceiling in your room and work your way down to the floor. This way any dust from above will collect with dust in sections below and you'll clean it up once. If you clean the opposite way, from the bottom up, you'll most likely have dust from the ceiling fall on your newly clean floor and you'll just have to clean it over again. Now that you know this timesaving tip, here are some items to make sure to keep clean:

Check Ceiling Cobwebs	Dust Chandelier/Fans	Inspect & Clean Skylights
Dust Walls	Wipe Windows/Sills	Wash Curtains/Blinds
Wipe Doors/Doorways	Shine All Woodwork	Wipe Wall Art/Photos
Clean Mirrors	Dust Shelves/Built-In	Clean Behind Furniture
Vacuum/Steam Clean	Dust Furniture Surfaces	Wash Pillows/Blankets
Lint Roll Lamp Shades	Wipe Baseboards	Clean Fireplace
Mop Tile	Clean/Replace Mats	Scrub Sinks
Wipe All Surfaces	Clean Grout	Shine Wood Floors

Pay close attention to the rooms you use frequently in your home, such as the kitchen and the bathroom. These two rooms are also high on a buyer's wish list, so take your time and make sure they sparkle. By doing so, you'll show buyers that you take pride in your home.

Another important factor to remember when tidying up is to use your sense of smell. We've all come across homes where you just wanted to hold your nose and run out the door screaming. Who can blame you—the sense of smell is the strongest of all the senses, especially when selling a home. The scents and odors in a home can connect or disconnect buyers to a house with just one sniff.

There is a reason why a home seller isn't aware of the urine smell or last night's dinner odor haunting the air. They're immune to the odor in their home. As a home stager, I've smelled my share of "stinky homes" from pets, food, clothes or shoes, smoking, mold, appliances, and air vents. When preparing a home for sale I recommend clients get rid of the sources of bad odor rather than simply mask the scent. Here are a few ways to tackle these unwanted smells:

Pets. Simply having a pet can create allergy flare-ups for some buyers. While on the housing market make sure to brush and give your animals a bath regularly. One of the worst smelling offenses is pet urine and feces. Clean litter boxes every other day. If your animal has been using your floor as a toilet, make sure to steam clean carpets and/or replace wood where it's damaged.

Food. Cooking food can create lingering odors in a home. When cooking, use stovetop fans and open a window. Wipe down hard surfaces and wash drapery and other fabrics around the kitchen. After cooking, make sure to dispose of trash outside immediately to avoid lingering smells. A tip: leave out ground coffee or vinegar in a bowl so it can absorb some of the unwanted smells. The best way to avoid food smells is not to cook with fish and spices like curry or ethnic foods with potent odors while on the housing market. Go out to dinner for those foods if you have a craving.

Clothes or Shoes. Smelly socks, sports equipment, shirts, or shoes—anything that has perspiration on it—will eventually create a stink. Make sure to wash linens and clothing on a regular basis; don't let it pile up when selling. Try leaving shoes outside to air. Also, use Febreeze on bigger items that can't be put in the wash.

Smoke. Cigarette smoke is hard to get rid of without completely painting the room, wiping down hard surfaces, removing fabrics and carpets. Smoke imbedded in walls can be contained by using a high-quality primer prior to painting. When selling your house you must stop smoking in your home. Smoke sticks to everything, even light bulbs. Then when the light is on and heats up, the scent will return. In this case, keep the light bulb clean and it won't be a problem. Also, try leaving a bowl of vinegar out for twenty-four hours prior to a showing to remove the smell of cigarette smoke (this won't help heavy smokers).

Mold. Mold smells are a huge red flag for buyers. Take care of musty or moldy smells immediately with a dehumidifier, or kill mold spores using chlorine dioxide. If it's extremely bad, hire a professional. You can use a company like www.servpro.com. If they're not in your area, check www.angieslist.com.

Appliances. Buyers will open refrigerators, especially if it's something that comes with the house. Make sure to remove smelly or rotten food from the fridge at least once a week. Use a box of baking soda to absorb odors in the fridge, and wipe down shelves when needed. Appliances throughout the house should also be cleaned on a monthly basis, including ovens, dishwashers, and washers.

Air Vents. Change the filters in any ventilation, heating, or air conditioning system. Those systems work better when the filters are regularly cleaned anyway, and if you're trying to get rid of odors, there's no sense having them circulate in your ventilation system. Also, check air vents and wall outlets as an odor source. You may have a dead mouse or something else in the wall causing a stink.

Once you address the source of the odors, you want to make sure the space smells clean during open houses. A clean smell and a deodorized smell are two different things though. Pulling out scented candles and plug-ins or preparing baked cookies may smell nice to some, but others may think you're masking a smell or could find the scent appalling. Even worse, the scent could distract the buyer's ability to make a decision.

According to a recent study in the *Journal of Retailing*[7], shoppers spent 31.8 percent more when a store was scented with a simple orange scent over a complex blend of scents. The study recommends using simple scents such as orange, lemon, basil, vanilla, green tea, pine, and cedar. These scents are easier to sort out, less distracting, and thus more conducive to spending. When deciding what scent works best for your home, take a cue from your location. For example, you can use pine and cedar scents for a house in the woods, but not at the beach.

One of my favorite scents is called citrus cilantro from Pier 1 Imports. It comes in sprays, candles, and oils. Whatever smell you decide on, remember to first find the source of the smell; if you can't smell it recruit a friend to take a sniff. Then take care of the smell appropriately. Finally, infuse new scents into the home to enhance buyer interest.

Now, I understand cleaning isn't really a fun thing to be doing with your time, but I promise you it will make a huge impact in selling your home. So, since it's an important part of the selling process, why not make it fun? Turn up the music, get all family members involved, and come up with a desirable reward. Maybe it's giving the kids an allowance, maybe it's buying that pair of shoes you've had your eye on, or maybe it's taking the entire family out to dinner or for ice cream. Use whatever reward necessary to motivate the cleaning process and eventually you'll be able to change your habits about the way you clean. Hey, you may even end up becoming a clean freak! For more cleaning tips visit my Pinterest page at www.pinterest.com/toritothstager/cleanfreak.

---

7   Journal of Retailing, Volume 89, Issue 1, March 2013, Pages 30-43

Step 7: Highlight positive features to showcase an aspiring lifestyle

Every room has positive and negative features; it's what you do with those features that can make a buyer excited about your space. In any room of the house there should be a dramatic focal point that attracts your eye, but is that focal point pleasing to the eye? Does it have a positive connotation or a negative one? These are questions I asked you to answer in the buyer's exercise, where you went through each room of your home and assessed the space. If you haven't done this yet, stop, go through each room, and take notes of the positive and negative features around your home.

You may be asking, *Well, Tori, what is a positive and negative feature in a home?* It's different in every home, but here's a list of some positive features you may have in your home:

Positive Features
- Large Front Yard
- Landscaping/Sprinkler Systems
- Two-Car Garage
- Deck/Patio
- Swimming Pool
- Outdoor Living Area
- Outdoor View
- Energy-Efficient Windows/Insulation/Appliances
- Picture Windows/Sliding or French Doors
- Grand Foyer
- Wood Floors
- Built-in Shelving
- Fireplace
- Hi-Hat Lighting/Fans/Chandeliers
- Lots of Storage Space/Closets
- Kitchen with Island

- Home Office
- Master Suite with Spa-Like Bathroom
- Large Rooms
- Family Room or Additional Great Room
- Open Layout
- Finished Basement

These are just a few of the positive features buyers look for in a new home. If you have these types of features in your home, guess what? You're one step closer to the closing table because you already own what buyers are looking for. Now you just have to make sure they notice those features. Before I get into how to highlight these positive features, I want to share with you a list of negative features, or basically anything that is an eyesore, a needed repair, or an imperfection you can't change.

Negative Features

- Location of Home
- Uninviting Curb Appeal
- No Garage
- Unappealing or No Landscape
- Peeling Exterior Paint/Bad Paint Colors
- Old Roof
- Old Windows/Doors
- Small or Awkward Layout
- Carpeting
- Outdated Kitchen and Bathrooms
- Small Bedrooms
- Limited Ceiling Lighting
- Structural Problems
- Electrical/Plumbing Problems

Some of these negative features can have a real impact on whether the buyer makes an offer or not, and if an offer is made how much will they take off the sales price to budget in improving these features? As I mentioned before, some features are just out of your control; for instance, the location of your home is impossible to change.

My home is in a remote location in South Queens, in the same neighborhood where a home's price tag can easily be over $1 million. My home is steps away from Jamaica Bay, which is great for boaters and summertime activities, plus it has easy access to transportation and shops. The problem with my home's location is that it's beneath a JFK flight path, so we constantly hear planes. In fact, I can see the JFK control tower from my bedroom window. After living here for ten years the planes don't bother me anymore, but it could bother a potential buyer.

Now, with that said, any home in my area whether it's $300,000 or $1.5 million hears these planes, so if the buyer wants to live in my neighborhood they have to deal with this noise. If you have an impossible negative feature like this plaguing your home, just make sure to acknowledge it and refocus buyers on the positive aspects, such as the fact that this is a great beach town or on other features you can change.

So, in order to make sure these positive features get noticed, we have to downplay the negative aspects of the space. Stylish Stagers staged a co-op apartment in Kew Gardens that is a great example of this. The space was average; nothing really grabbed the buyer's attention. And while the apartment was large, the seller's belongings were scattered everywhere. This picture was their living room before we staged the space. What attracts your eye? Is it positive or negative?

The orange focal wall stands out and says, "look at me," but there is nothing there to look at. While the window is large and bright, the curtains are less than attractive. The paint color also directs your eye to that door in the corner. This door had caused many headaches for the sellers because it's a door to nowhere. They'd been on the market for a year before calling us, and the sellers said, "Every time a buyer comes in they question that door." So we knew we'd need to come up with a solution. Take a look at what we did.

Client's living room in Kew Gardens, Queens. What is positive or negative in this space?

Kew Gardens living room after staging.

Our company painted the room a comfy beige, removed their window treatment, and added curtains from floor to ceiling, flanking the picture window. Then we extended the fabric to cover the doorway. Presto, the door to nowhere is now nowhere to be found. We also switched the furniture layout so that when you walked through the front door into the room you saw the couch rather than the entertainment center. As you can see, by painting, decluttering, rearranging, and adding some modern accessories by taking a cue from mother nature, we were able to update this two-bedroom, two-bath co-op and highlight many of the space's positive areas, such as picture windows, spacious layout, and wood floors.

Understanding focal points is an important part of the staging process, but it can sometimes be hard for an untrained eye to determine what a focal point is and how to use it effectively. A focal point is usually defined by what the purpose of the room will be. Focal points can come in many shapes and sizes; in fact, there can be many focal points in the same room competing against one another.

There are three different types of focal points, each important to showcase:

Natural Focal Point. This focal point has to deal with location and the natural elements surrounding your home. Does your home have a view buyers desire? If so, you want to highlight the windows framing the view, because it can increase the value of your home.

Architectural Focal Point. This type of focal point relates to manmade features like built-ins throughout your home. A fireplace, bookcase, or bay window with these types of features fits into this category. Now if you don't have any natural or architectural focal points, there is another way to attract a buyer's eye with what I call a creative focal point.

Creative Focal Point. This is when you physically create a focal point with items such as paint, furniture, and accessories to direct the buyer's eye. This can be done by painting the focal wall a shade darker or placing a couch on the focal wall with artwork above. In most cases, you will have to create a focal point in each room, so let's talk a bit more on how to do this: What is the first thing you see when you walk into the room? What is the first wall you see? It's usually the one opposite to the entrance to the room. Is what you see positive or negative?

Determine the function of the room. Is it the living room? A bedroom? What is this room used for?

Based on the function of the room, what is the focal point? In a bedroom, a bed. In an office, a desk, etc. Figure out if you have any natural or architectural focal points to highlight, then determine the furniture needed to create your own focal points.

When choosing your focal point, you want it to have a huge impact and get buyer's attention. You can do this by using color, texture, or hanging vertical pieces on the wall to emphasize a room's height.

Once you've determined the focal point, you want that to take center stage to anything else in the room. So if you have a fireplace in a room, make sure the furniture faces toward the fireplace. Or in a bedroom, the focal point is the bed, and you can place a chair or seating area facing toward the bed.

Remember, whatever your focal point is, it should be placed on your focal wall so buyers can instantly see this positive feature and know what this room is used for.

Focal Points Room by Room. Every room has a different focal point, so to save time and your sanity, I have provided a cheat sheet of the most common focal points used in each room. Once you've defined your focal point and cleared clutter, keep a minimum of three feet of wall space on either side of the focal point empty to ensure that it stands out. If you need to add furniture or accessories around your focal point, make sure they are cohesive and balanced with like items in the space to avoid distracting buyers from the focal point.

Entryway
- Table that is proportionate to space
- Artwork or Mirror
- Seating Area

Living Room
- Fireplace (Usually Main Focal)
- Picture or Bay Windows with View
- Couch with Artwork Above
- TV

Dining Room
- Dining Table
- Table Centerpieces
- Chandelier

Office
- Desk
- Built-in Bookcase

Kitchen

- Island
- Stove Hood
- Sink Area
- Tiling/Countertops

Bedroom

- Bed with Artwork Above (Main Focal)
- Extra Seating Area

Bathroom

- Bathtub
- Shower
- Vanity and Sink Area

Let's look at an example of how to enhance a focal point. The photos below are of a bedroom in a one-bedroom apartment in the Meatpacking District of New York City. Take a look at the before photos; they had so many items flanking the focal wall: a large plant, a nightstand, a bed, an extremely large photo, a crib, a floor lamp, and a changing table. Does that bedroom look like it would be comfortable to sleep in? Would you buy this home based on this room? Probably not. It looks cluttered, lacks storage, and the focal point is getting lost in translation.

Photo of a bedroom, located on West 23rd Street, NYC, before staging.   *Photo of same bedroom, after the home was staged by our company, Summer 2013.*

Check out the transformation. There is an incredible difference between the before and after photos. You can clearly determine the focal point, which is the bed. We've highlighted the bed by pairing matching nightstands, table lamps, and photos. The bed is also located on the focal wall, so it's the first thing you notice when entering the room. The staged bedroom looks relaxing, like a hotel room. Buyers noticed too, and after staging, the apartment sold in less than thirty days.

Competing Focal Points. As I mentioned before, in some rooms you may have competing focal points. Let's say in a master bedroom you have a fireplace and a bed. Which one is the main focal point? In a bedroom, it is the bed. Let's say you have a living room with a fireplace and sliding glass doors that lead to a deck looking off a canal. Which one is the main focal point? They're both equally important, so you want to try to create a furniture layout that will showcase both. What if you have a fireplace in the living room and a large-screen TV? You want to move the TV closer to the fireplace, ideally above the fireplace or on either side. This way both focal points are in the same area and won't have buyers' eyes fighting over which way to look.

To sell your home for maximum value, you need to subliminally keep the focus of each buyer that walks in the door. Start by working through this section of the book, and create a list of positive and negative features. Figure out how you can enhance the positive features and downplay the negative features. Don't worry about features that are beyond your control. Then list all the things you love about your home. Think back to when you bought the home. What were the reasons you decided to buy? What made you feel at home in the space? Consider how your house works for different family members as well. Is there a way to capture that in a creative focal point? By thinking back to those times, you can start to create a lifestyle buyers will want.

Step 8: Optimize space to enhance square footage

Buyers are looking to purchase a certain amount of square footage to call home, so you need to maximize the space in your home so that each room not only appears bigger but has dual functionality to enhance buyer appeal. You can do this by decluttering, lighting up the room, and of course having a spacious furniture layout. The layout will determine the visual size and flow of the room. Take note of how the furniture is placed in your house. Is there a focal point in each room? Are there easy pathways around the furniture? Arranging furniture is an important step in home staging because it dictates how the buyer will visually see the space. As a home stager, I avoid overwhelming the room with furniture. Rather, I focus on strategically placing furniture around the room that will enhance the positive features and space available in the furniture layout.

Here is a living room we staged in Manhattan. Can you figure out what the problems are in this before photo? This wall is the focal wall in the room, and everything is butted up against this wall except the main focal point, the couch. In this picture, the wall looks busy, the hutch is too big for that area, and there is clutter in every nook and cranny.

Before staging, a cluttered living room in Manhattan with a layout that lacked space.

Manhattan living room after staging. We switched the layout and removed the clutter.

We had the sellers pack up their belongings and remove the hutch. We repositioned the sofa on the focal wall, adding photos above to direct buyers' eyes as they walked into the home. The focal point now has breathing room on either side due to the new layout. In this furniture layout, we faced a chair toward the sofa to create a conversation area. Guests can also redirect the countertop stools to join in on the conversation. There is also ample room to walk around the coffee table to get to the outdoor patio. On the opposite wall, we added storage and a place to watch TV. This layout works better because it gives you a beautiful focal point, an ideal traffic pattern, and utilizes every square inch of space in the room, while leaving empty space for the eye to rest and process the layout.

Before furnishing any room, a homeowner should draw out the floor plan of their room, including the placement of windows and doors. Every room should invite you in, rather than stop you from entering. That's why you must pay attention to the traffic patterns in your home. Use these tips to create an ideal traffic pattern when placing furniture in the room:

Doorway Locations. Obviously you can't block a doorway, so if you have one doorway, you want to make sure seating is easily accessible. Put seating on either side of the doorway and don't put the couch's back toward the doorway; this makes the space feel uninviting. If you have two doorways in your room, consider having the traffic pattern move behind the seating areas rather than through it.

Furniture Placement. Start with your biggest piece of furniture, which is usually a couch. If you have natural or architectural focal points in the room, then you can place the couch on the longest wall available. If your room lacks focal points, place the couch on the focal wall or the first wall you see when you walk into the room. If your couch is placed off the wall, make sure to have at least three feet of walking space behind it.

Hazardous Edges. Try using tables with round edges to avoid hitting them. An oval coffee table can create a more comfortable flow in the traffic pattern.

Space. Some rooms are small and there is only one way in and one way out. If you have a limited traffic pattern, just make sure you're able to access what is needed to achieve your goals easily in that room. Make sure there is enough empty space for the buyer to get from point A to point B, with no obstacles in the traffic pattern.

Off the Wall. Avoid placing all your furniture up against the walls. Create multiple seating areas by positioning furniture off the wall. Have furniture face each other to create a conversation area. When you stack all your items up against the wall, it can feel awkward to sit, talk, or watch TV in the space.

Furniture Choices. These days furniture is larger and comes in a package deal: the more you buy the more you save. But this deal can be a deal breaker for homebuyers when they walk into your home and find your living space filled with furniture. When setting up your rooms, make sure to avoid having too much or not enough furniture in the space. Also, have the right scale of furniture that fits in the room easily, and create multiple seating areas that justify the function of the room. Move unneeded pieces to the garage or a storage unit.

Another way to optimize space in your home to enhance square footage is to make sure each room is balanced on either side. The balance of a room is determined by the placement of furniture and the size of each piece. If all the large pieces are on one side of the room, the space will feel off-balanced horizontally. The space can also be off-balance vertically if the furniture is too bottom-heavy or top-heavy. An example of bottom-heavy furniture can be a couch that sits close to the floor or a secretary's desk. Anything with visual weight will be considered bottom-heavy.

In contrast, top-heavy can be defined as furniture that has visual height, long legs, and empty space near the floor. So the balance of the room can be affected by the height, width, and weight of the objects collectively. In order to create balance throughout the room, use a floor plan of your space and section it off into four areas like this:

Separate the plan into four quadrants by drawing a horizontal and vertical line connecting in the middle of the room. Once you've drawn the lines, make sure there is an even amount of furniture and accessory items in each section of the room to avoid having an off-balanced or lopsided room. Balanced relationships between objects can be either symmetrical or asymmetrical. You can balance the same (symmetrical) or different but equally weighted objects throughout the room (asymmetrical). To bring balance and stability to your room, consider these following questions:

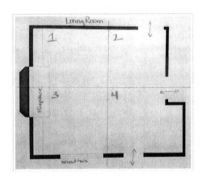

An Example of How to Section Off Your Floor Plan to Create Balance in the Room

- How does the height, width, and depth of each piece relate to the others in the room? Do you have two high pieces next to each other? If so, move them across from one another.
- Have you balanced a vertical piece, like a bookcase, wall unit, or windows, with another taller piece on the opposite side of the room?
- How tall are your windows and doorways? Make sure to consider them when arranging furniture, and mirror the height on an opposite wall if possible.

- Is your upholstered furniture similar in height? Do you have a mixture of seating that is bottom-heavy and top-heavy?
- Do you have large and small furnishings distributed evenly throughout the space?
- Can you balance two pieces of furniture by placing them on opposite walls diagonally across from one another?
- Does the room feel balanced and comfortable? Does anything stick out that should be removed?

The number of items in a room can also affect balance. A room with too much furniture can crowd a room and confuse buyers, while a room with no furniture may have buyers scratching their heads trying to figure out whether their furniture will fit there and how they will position it. Only 10 percent of buyers can visualize the potential of a space, so you don't want your deal to fall flat because the buyer had no imagination. By creating balance in your room, you will once again direct the buyer's eye.

In 2012, our company staged model units in this new-construction multi-unit building that stands eight stories high at Lexington Avenue and 104th Street in East Harlem. The building features one- and two-bedroom units with balconies, modern kitchens, baths, hardwood floors, and large windows. The apartment was completely empty when we staged the space. We brought in furnishings and accessories on a tight budget to enhance the look of the home. The space appeared smaller without furniture, so we wanted to make

Living and dining room area at an East Harlem home that was vacant prior to staging. We brought in furnishings to showcase a particular lifestyle.

sure we used every square inch of the home to show buyers the potential lifestyle they could have if they bought this home. Here is the living room and dining room area of the two-bedroom apartment.

I want to explain to you the reasoning behind our furniture choices and why we decided to set up the room this way. We obviously needed a place to lounge and entertain guests, but we also needed a place to eat besides the kitchen island. When you walk into the space, the first wall you notice is where the TV unit and dining table are located. So that wall became our focal wall; it was the longest wall in the room and was also able to flank the dining table. The opposite wall couldn't do that because it ended at the edge of the side table in the lower right-hand corner of the picture. The space was too small to add a chair opposite the couch to create a conversation area, so we decided to get a couch with a chaise for ample seating.

Since the wall unit is on the focal wall, I wanted it to make a statement. I chose this wall unit because the dark color would make it stand out, it had visual weight, plus it had lots of storage for buyers. I mimicked that color on the opposite wall with the side table, creating a sense of balance. If you notice, everything else in the room is a neutral color.

Since the wall unit is tall, I needed to create that same height on the opposite wall, which I did with the picture over the couch. And because the wall unit and couch are bottom-heavy, I chose a glass coffee table, which appears light, almost invisible, so it's not distracting from the focal point.

Now, all the furniture I've mentioned so far has straight edges, so I chose a round dining table to separate the two spaces, creating a flow right into the next space and avoiding any corners or sharp edges. Where else did I use a round shape? I softened the living room with polk-a-dot pillows and drum lamp shades. I also separated the two spaces by adding a rug in the living room area. Take notice of the traffic pattern as well. A buyer can easily access the balcony and walk around the coffee table to sit.

Think of this photo when trying to balance your room. Every quadrant in the room has furniture and a purpose. Each piece of furniture has empty space around it to help move the buyer's eye around the room.

Creating a Conversation Area

When putting together a furniture layout in your room, it's also important to think about the conversation area. Once you establish this area, the rest of the room falls into place because it usually helps establish a focal point and a traffic pattern. The goal of a conversation area is to arrange furniture so that people can sit facing one another and not have to yell across the room. When creating a conversation area, consider these following questions:

- Have you removed all irrelevant furnishings that don't fit in the conversation area? You should be able to walk through furniture arrangements easily.

- Did you use an area rug to define the space? Make sure to place a rug big enough so at least each piece of furniture's front legs rest on it.

- Is your couch positioned on the longest wall or focal wall, opposite the room's entrance? This is important.

- Is there seating across from or on the sides of the couch for people to talk face-to-face? We want to create a place for people to gather.

- Have you strategically placed tables around the seating area for people to use? Is there a coffee table in the middle of the seating area? People need a surface to place items on.

- Sit in the space. Do you have to turn your head or body to make eye contact with someone? If so, you need to reposition the furniture.

- I suggest you try a few different layouts either on paper or by moving the furniture around to see what traffic patterns work best by strategically placing furniture to create balance and conversation areas throughout the space. To see an example of this from start to finish you can check out this video at www.toritoth.com/home-staging-arranging-furniture. Please post your questions or furniture layout success stories and photos on our Facebook fan page at www.facebook.com/ homestagingtips.

We're almost finished learning the FEEL AT HOME process, those ten steps all homeowners should complete before listing their home. Next let's take a look at how décor plays a role in attracting buyers.

Step 9: Modify decor by updating the look of your home

Once you have the furniture in place, it's time to decorate the space, which means to make something look more attractive by adding extra items or images to the room. As you're decorating your new space, don't put all the same accessories back in the same room in the same place. This defeats the purpose of staging, and you may not make a major impact on the space if you return all your old items to the room. Instead, marry the old with the new to create a lifestyle buyers will want to aspire to.

Let me warn you: it's a subconscious habit to put items back in their old places, because that's just what you're used to. So be aware of the habit, think about the buyer, use your creativity, and break the pattern.

When trying to modify your decor, take your accessories piece by piece to see if you can actually use them in your space. At this point you need to depersonalize your home by removing those accessories that are all about you. Depersonalizing your home allows buyers to envision themselves living in the house. When buyers see your personal photos or collectibles displayed in the house, the only person they can imagine in the house is you. So pack, remove, or store the following:

- School Awards, Certificates, and Medals
- Collectibles/Figurines
- Toys (try to keep them in kid's room or toy room)
- DVDs, Video Games, and CDs
- Excess Magazines/Newspapers
- Mail/Paperwork
- Fridge Magnets
- Sticky Notes/Calendars (can keep in an office area)
- Kid's Artwork
- Medications
- Beauty and Bath Products
- Photographs

Yes, I said photographs, but not all of them. When you're trying to sell your home, you want to remove photos to give buyers a chance to envision themselves living there, but it also helps avoid distracting buyers. When buyers visit homes, they can easily be distracted by photos. They may even wind up being more interested in who lives there than in the positive features of the home. Remember, you want to keep buyers focused when they're considering your home. They need to remember the large great room, not the people who live in it. So any pictures that are head shots or full-body shots like school, graduation, or wedding photos need to be removed.

Not all photographs have to be put away, however. Some are worthy of staying out while on the market. Action photos or photos that can showcase the potential lifestyle your buyers are looking to acquire can actually benefit the sale. What do I mean by this? If you have pictures that capture fun moments in time or things buyers can experience while living in your area, like hiking, boating, a day at the beach, or skiing, then frame and display them. By showcasing these action pictures that demonstrate an appealing lifestyle experience, buyers will be reminded of what their life will be like if they live there.

By editing your decor and depersonalizing, you have made room for new accessories that can lure in your target buyer. Remember, you don't want to choose new accessories specific to your taste, you want to use decor that expresses the personality of the potential buyer. That's why it's important to research the buyer's demographics and psychographics. This step includes a small investment in purchasing or repurposing accessories and artwork, but it allows you to instantly modernize your space with the buyer in mind. Place only a few key decorative elements near the focal points of each room. Using a minimal amount of decor pieces will allow buyers to see the house and get excited about the life they could lead by signing the contract. Follow these simple design rules when decorating your room:

- Strategically place accessories to enhance focal points, connect two objects together, and direct the buyer's eye.
- Group accessories in odd numbers to make it look more appealing.
- Group accessories according to height, function style, or color to keep it visually interesting, everything the same is boring.
- Repeat colors, textures, and paired items throughout the space, so the eye connects from one object to another.
- Take a cue from nature. Bring in wood, organic material accessories, flowers, and plants. It softens the entire space and makes it feel a bit more cozy and comfortable.

- Use accessories larger than a softball to make it feel less cluttered and allow each piece to make its own statement.
- Pay close attention to detail to avoid distracting buyers.
- Add something unexpected that will draw the buyer's attention.
- Create a cohesive theme throughout the room with matching accessories to showcase the space as a whole.
- Mix and match colors and patterns to create textural layers.
- Experiment with flowers. Use one type of flower and put them in individual pots, or use a bouquet of flowers to add life to a space.

Using key decor pieces is crucial to creating a cohesive feel that will make buyers feel at home. We used this technique when staging a home at the Landmark building in New York City. This growing family needed to revamp their home. With little luck selling their space overlooking the Queensborough Bridge, they changed realtors and brought in our company, Stylish Stagers, to stage their two-bedroom, two-bath home. We brought in color, a privacy solution for the balconies, plus we gave them alternative ways to store their kids' daily accessories.

In the living room, we reused their furniture and rug. We brought in colorful pillows,

Living room before staging at the Landmark, NYC.

Staging transformation of the living room. We used color, added small furnishings, and reused what they had to complete the look.

tabletop accessories, a small table, and a coffee table that doubled as a storage trunk for the kids' toys. Do you see how accessories can complete the look of this room?

Here's a look at the master bedroom we staged in this home. Take a look at this room: it appears dark, dingy, and old with no real decor emphasizing the space.

We kept their bedroom furniture, the table lamps, and the upholstered bench at the bottom of the bed. Since the fabric in the

Before photo of bedroom at the Landmark, NYC. Flower power was making this bedroom look old, dingy, and dark. The room also appears disorganized.

Here's the bedroom after staging it with key accessories.

seating matched the pillows, we took a cue from those colors and brought in a neutral bedspread. It was important to organize the clutter on the nightstands and make the overall room appear brighter. We did that by adding mirrors behind their table lamps, which was able to reflect the light throughout the room. We repeated the color red in the flowers, pillow, and blanket, which matches the rose pattern in the existing fabric.

As you're updating your home with decor, pay attention to detail. As a home stager, I've seen my share of inappropriate accessories and cockeyed wall hangings displayed as an afterthought. When you're selling your house, you want to think of home accessories as "jewelry" for your room. You wouldn't wear ten rings on your fingers, would you? So why have ten pieces of artwork haphazardly hanging on the wall or placed on a shelf? When selling your home, the golden rule is "less is more."

Bookcases and Shelving. Arranging a bookcase is actually an art form that focuses on colors, balance, and space. Take a look at your display cases and shelves around your home. Do they look cluttered? Are they filled with collectibles or knickknacks? Do you have items displayed that are smaller than a softball? If so, you're going to want to prepare your shelves for maximum visual impact.

Make sure your shelves have a purpose and display the lifestyle potential buyers will have in this home. Take one room at a time and remove all items from the shelves. Determine if any of these shelves can become a functional space, such as a wine bar, coffee bar, or desk. Then shop around your home to see if you can use items throughout your house.

If your bookcase's paint is peeling or the shelves need an update, try painting the unit to make this a positive feature in the room. You can also add temporary peel-and-stick wallpaper or fabric on foam board for shelves' backs to draw in the buyer's eyes.

When displaying books, pack away any paperback books and books with clothbound covers this way your books will provide a cleaner appearance on the shelf. You may even want to cover the books in white or colorful paper to create symmetry throughout the entire display case. Next, figure out what's going back on the shelf based on your room's theme, the design style (is it contemporary or traditional?), and the lifestyle you're promoting. Here is a list of tips to use when trying to create a bookcase or shelves that will impact a buyer:

- Remove clutter and small items to refrain from distracting buyers.

- Create variety by playing with visual height and weight to help the buyer's eyes move throughout the room.
- Use different textured items and mixed materials to enhance buyer interest.
- Choose colors that will work with one another. Play with the color wheel; choose colors on the same side of the color wheel or opposite sides for high impact.
- Experiment with symmetry of the items being used. Pairs can make buyers feel more relaxed because they've already seen the item once in the room.
- Pay close attention to the season and time of year you're selling in and use decor that showcases the current season.
- Use different shapes on the shelves to create some character.
- Use books to display decor at different heights.
- Have enough empty space for the eye to rest.
- Every object should feel as though it belongs to the composition and has purpose.

Empty shelves leave buyers wondering what to do with this space.

Shelves after staging. We brought in kitchen accessories to display and created a functional space to store coffee, toast food, and hold glasses.

Remember, stand back to look at the shelf and make sure it's visually appealing. When working with more than one shelf in the same area, look at the composition of the entire display case. Add a combination of books, decorative items, functional spaces, and some empty spaces for the eye to rest. The entire space should tell a story, look uncluttered, and have balance between the items on the shelves. Here's an example of shelving in a kitchen that the homeowner wasn't utilizing. We brought in key accessories to accentuate this space.

Hanging Artwork. Artwork, like display cases, can direct the buyer's eye, so make sure to strategically place artwork in key places throughout each room. Do you have a large piece of artwork next to a small piece? Do you have a shelf hung too high? What about artwork grouped too close together? You want the artwork to make a room's focal point stand out. First, remove all the artwork from the walls and determine if the art represents your target market based on location, type of buyer, and design style.

Once you've chosen the artwork, which could also be a mirror, tapestry, or ironwork, decide where to hang it based on the room's purpose. For instance, a landscape should be hung in a living room or family room rather than a kitchen, where a piece of fruit or floral arrangement should be showcased. Hanging artwork too high or too low can distract buyers, so as a home stager, I recommend hanging artwork four to ten inches above an object such as a sofa or table. If there is no furniture on the wall, hang the center of a large piece of art fifty-six to sixty inches from the floor. When grouping artwork together, distance the pieces one to three inches apart from each other. Use these home staging tips to avoid catching your buyers off guard because a distracted buyer won't be a serious buyer and make an offer:

- Hang items that may be unconventional: baskets, ironwork, ceramics, empty frames, etc. Be creative and think outside the box.

- Group artwork together when you need a large piece but don't have one available. It will take up more wall space and bring it up to scale with the rest of the room.
- If you're grouping artwork, try to use something repetitive like the frames, mattes, or black-and-white images versus colored photos so it appears to be one large piece.
- Pay attention to size, balance, color, and texture of the artwork so that it fits in with the design style.
- Artwork should be no more than two-thirds the size of the furniture it's placed above. We don't want artwork floating around the room, we want it to emphasize the space.
- Use the proper wall-hanging tools. Do you need wire, hooks, nails, anchors, or screws? This will prevent the artwork from falling off the wall.
- Drill a hole in plastered or concrete walls to hang artwork with ease.
- Here are a few different examples of how you can add artwork along your walls:
- Play around with what you have and purchase artwork that will enhance the overall lifestyle you're trying to create for buyers.

In this picture: Top left, we used wood sunburst mirrors to create a focal point over the dining table. We placed them to lead the eye into the TV. Top right, another way we added the TV into the focal wall, we made it a piece of artwork and strategically placed art on either side and used a wall decal saying, "life is simple," which subliminally talks to buyers about the type of life they could have living here. Bottom left, we created art with fake flowers and plants and spray paint. We then matted and framed them in the same frames and placed them in a horizontal line to show the size of the dining room. Middle right, this bedroom is highlighted by two pieces of ironwork. We hung it to reflect one large piece. Bottom right, even a simple large piece of artwork over the couch can direct the eye.

Examples of how to hang artwork in your home.

Rugs. Don't forget to add some bling to your floor with a rug. Rugs can be a bit of a mystery and fairly challenging, especially when purchasing the proper size. The goal is to use a rug that contains colors in the room that you want to emphasize. A rug can make a space feel warm and inviting, but most importantly it can define a room. It can also instantly update a space. Many homeowners use rugs ineffectively; that's why I thought it was important to address here. The first thing you want to do when purchasing a rug is to measure the size of the room. Keep in mind that the larger an area rug is, the more spacious the room will seem to be. Avoid using rugs smaller than 5x7 unless you're using it as a utility rug, and make sure the rug you choose has a purpose. Here are some tips to think about when purchasing a new rug:

- Use an area rug to anchor furniture. Make sure to have at least part of the furniture resting on the rug.
- 5x7 or 8x10 rugs are the most acceptable for living rooms and bedrooms.
- In a bedroom, it's ideal to have the rug halfway under the bed.
- In a dining room, rugs should be at least two feet larger than the table. This way when you pull out the chairs, they still remain on the rug.
- Avoid random rugs; rugs shouldn't be alone unless they're used in an entryway or hallway.
- It's okay to have only the front legs of furniture on the rug in a living room arrangement.
- Make sure your rug matches the style of the room (contemporary or traditional).
- Add some contrast to the flooring. Use a light-colored rug on dark floors and vice versa.
- Warm up spaces with rugs.
- Use a textured rug like sisal, shag, plush, or fur style.
- Divide a large open space with a rug.
- Think about adding a rug on top of carpet to define a conversation area. The key to this is to make sure the rug has a pattern.

Remember, use an area rug as a decorative piece that defines a room and adds instant warmth. Find the perfect affordable rug in all shapes, sizes, and textures at these stores: www.rugsusa.com, Target, and IKEA.

Many designers say start with the area rug first when coming up with a design plan. From the rug, you can choose colors to paint your walls and find throw pillows and paintings to complete the decor. As a rule, the area rug should be no less than six inches away from the wall and no more than two feet away from the wall; however, rules are made to be broken. Take into consideration the different uses and shapes when placing the rug. For instance, in this bedroom (below) we used a faux-cowhide rug. It has a shape that is distinctive, so I didn't want the bed to cover up the rug completely. We chose to put the rug near the door. This way buyers noticed it right away and it created a warm cozy feel. We then played with the colors of the rug and used a rich brown in the bedding.

This Long Island living room already had a colorful couch, so we used an off-white textured rug.

This room had a green-gray couch, so we used a neutral 5x7 rug to complete the look of the furniture arrangement. We also decided to use a textured rug to bring in some depth. While the rug is rectangular, the pattern is circular, which matches the accent chairs, table lamps, sunburst mirror, and pillows.

Step 10: Exploit emotions to close the sale

Tip number ten of the FEEL AT HOME process is learning how to play with a buyer's emotions. We've all heard people say, "I fell in love with this home as soon as I walked in the door" or "After months of house hunting, I knew this was it!" Home buying is initially more of an emotional commitment than a financial one. Yes, you're unloading thousands of dollars in savings to fund the down payment and pay the mortgage, but the bottom line is that most homebuyers purchase first with their emotions and then justify the purchase with their wallets. Why? Because a home is several things: it's where you live, it's where you raise your family, it's a reflection of who you are—it's a status symbol!

Regardless of stress, anticipation, or in some cases frustration, the simple fact is a buyer can get attached to one home over another. That's why we need to make sure your home stays top of mind. You want the buyer to feel an emotional attachment to your home by visualizing themselves living there. They can't do that if they walk in on your cluttered mess. That's the reason I've created the 10 Steps to FEEL AT HOME process for you to follow. The nine steps leading up to this one—from first impressions and how to profile a buyer to decluttering—give you the tools needed so buyers won't feel they're intruding on your space.

To exploit a buyer's emotions you must first understand that these so-called feelings are a necessary ingredient in almost all decisions. When a buyer is confronted with a decision, emotions from previous or related experiences affix values to the options they are considering. These emotions create preferences that lead to the decision to buy.

Let's say a buyer's wish list includes having a formal dining room. This person isn't necessarily concerned about a place to put the dining room set, rather they're thinking of how great it will feel to have the entire family over for a holiday dinner. Feelings are what homebuyers are after; that's why when staging a home we're "telling a story," mindful of the dreams, aspirations, and lifestyle of the targeted buyer. Every piece of furniture, artwork, and accessory used is carefully selected to establish an emotional connection point with a buyer. You can create these emotional connection points by displaying moments in time that showcase what buyers will experience in each room of the home. Creating these scenes makes buyers subconsciously desire to live in your home.

So let's go room by room and talk about some of the ways you can add emotion to your newly decorated spaces and utilize the top ten positive emotions determined by Dr. Barbara Fredrickson, author of *Positivity: Research Reveals the 3 to 1 Ratio That Will Change Your Life*. A pioneer in studying positive emotions, she describes how the following ten positive emotions can increase your ability to move forward in life. Use these ten positive emotions, plus a few others, when preparing your home for sale to show buyers what they could feel (the emotions are listed in italics under each room category).

Entry hallway at home on Long Island prior to staging. The mirror was old and dingy. Is this welcoming for a buyer?

Entryway. This is the first room buyers see and it makes an impression on them in seconds. Make sure to transition the outside in with a plant, and start the walk-thru off with an accessory or two introducing the home's theme.

Welcoming — Make sure space smells fresh and is light and bright; add some flowers or a plant.

Joyful — Showcase life and energy (add pop of color).

Living Room. The living room is a place to entertain guests. This room is usually more formal and where the entire family comes together. Here you can let your design style shine, especially if it's the second room buyers see.

Same entry after staging. We removed the mirror, but it left a mark on the wall, so we painted a rectangle and hung a shelf and mirror inside to add some visual appeal. Notice how the accessories are joyful.

Awe — Offer the feeling of luxury when buyers walk through this room, remove inexpensive decor (add paintings, metals, glass, rich woods, and light-colored fabrics).

Warmth — Make the room feel warm with wall color, a rug, textured fabric, throws, and pillows. Even lighting your fireplace, candles, and ambient lighting can bring warmth to a room.

Elegance — Create a light and spacious room; use a few antiques and a symmetrical decor scheme. Worldly pieces from your travels are great to showcase in this room.

Family or Bonus Room. This type of room is less formal than a living room. It's a place where the family goes to hang out. Here you can be a bit more playful in your decor.

Here are some examples of emotional connection points in a family room. A buyer can play games like monopoly or chess, enjoy a cigar, or knit something comfy.

Amusement — The buyer should visualize where they can catch a sports game with friends, play board games with family, and cuddle up to watch a movie.

Surprise — Give buyers a surprise by showcasing how adults and kids can both enjoy this space.

Comfy — Use soft or fluffy textures, mix and match patterns and colors. Add natural elements, make sure there is ample seating, and take a cue from earth tones.

Dining Room. The main objective in this room is having good food, being entertained, and enjoying the company of family and friends.

Pride — In this room you want buyers to feel the pride they would experience when hosting a dinner party. People usually entertain because they want to show off their lifestyle. Maybe your buyer needs more space to throw parties, like a first-time homebuyer who could never imagine having a dinner party in a studio apartment. By viewing this space, they can visualize the goal of hosting a family event they never thought was attainable. So set the table for a party!

Belonging — By having a separate dining room and thinking about what this room will be used for, you get the feeling that you belong, that you fit in with the other people who will sit in these chairs around the table.

Love — Go one step further and imagine the love the homeowner will receive in this home: praise for an amazing meal or reminiscences over fond memories. You can show love by using color, adding family heirlooms, and using those lifestyle photos.

Kitchen. The kitchen is the heart of the home. It's not just a place where food is made, but is a place for families to come together. You can cook, do homework, entertain, or just hang out in the kitchen. Think about how many times you hang out in your kitchen. When I visit my neighbor, we always find ourselves sitting around the island chatting about the events in our lives. It's comfortable; make your kitchen feel like this. Think about entertaining friends, gourmet cooking, wine tasting, espresso drinking, and a luxurious, leisurely lifestyle when staging this space.

Here are examples of emotional connection points in a kitchen. A buyer can visualize where to research recipes, cook, get their morning coffee, or entertain guests.

Inspiration — Be organic! When a buyer sees your kitchen, they should feel inspired to cook. Add a cookbook, sparkling water, or fruits on display. This not only reminds them the cooking is done here, but that it's healthy cooking.

Anticipation — Get buyers to anticipate the amazing smells that can emanate from the kitchen. Display herbs on the countertop or windowsill, and let the aromas fill the room. Or light a food candle like gingerbread, cookie dough, or apple cinnamon.

Interest—— Since this is the heart of the home, get buyers to take interest in the daily activities that will take place here. Whether it's getting the family ready for school, organizing schedules over coffee, or having a wine tasting, set up these scenes to get buyers interested in this potential lifestyle.

Master Bedroom. Your master bedroom should feel like a hotel room. The room should house only a bedroom set and possibly a seating area. Everything else that you store in this room—an office, exercise equipment, laundry—should be removed or put away.

Serenity — A place to be at peace, relaxed and mellow. Use tranquil colors like blues, grays, or purple; make sure the room is clean, and use a relaxing smell like lavender. Take a cue from your favorite hotel room.

Luxurious — An adult space that has no distractions. The kids' toys, furniture, or other belongings shouldn't be in this room. Have textured

Here are examples of emotional connection points for a master bedroom. A buyer can see themselves relaxing in these rooms reading or enjoying tea time!

linens and throw pillows, and mix metals like gold and silver in decor to create the feel of luxury. In a bedroom you can show a family photo or two, place a few books on the nightstand, have fresh flowers, and allow a perfume or cologne display.

Bathroom. Think spa; what makes a spa so relaxing? Use that in your master bathroom and other baths in your home. This is where you may want to consider investing your money and get rid of those pink and blue bathrooms.

Calm — To create a calming emotion use earth tones or cool colors; remove all personal products and bath toys. Bring in spa soaps, bath salts, a few candles, and an orchid. Get a plush rug. Keep the overall look simple.

Here are examples of emotional connection points for extra bedrooms. Now a buyer can visualize what to do with the extra space depending on their needs.

Clean — Make sure the bathroom is clean and free from dirt, hair, and grime. Use white accents to emphasize cleanliness in towels and the shower curtain. Use soothing aromas like citrus cilantro, vanilla, or other fragrances you find in a spa.

Kids' Rooms/Office. These are extra rooms to portray the lifestyle of your home.

Optimism or Hope — Give the illusion of space so buyers will feel they can grow into the home. In many cases buyers are moving because they need more room for kids, work, or play. This is where you show them what they could do with this extra space. Make them see what the future could hold.

Overall. The house overall should flow together and get buyers excited, thinking *This is it, this is my home!*

Gratitude — By tapping into the buyer's emotion and staging a home, the buyer will feel gratitude toward you because you took the time to prepare your home for sale. Maybe the buyer has seen some horrible houses prior to viewing your listing, and this home lets them be thankful that their time house hunting wasn't wasted.

The hardest part of living in a home that's on the market is constantly being prepared to show the space. The more a seller does in advance to prepare and showcase the home by utilizing the 10 Steps to FEEL AT HOME process, the faster the property will sell. When it sells quickly, you as a homeowner can limit your time facing the negative emotions that derive from public scrutiny and having your lifestyle inconvenienced while on the market.

In the next chapter we'll sum everything up with three basic skills that will put you over the top in the competitive real estate market.

Chapter 7

THE PROSPEROUS PREPS:
THREE BROAD SKILLS FOR HOME SELLING SUCCESS

'm often asked, "What is it that you think about and consistently practice when staging a home?" This is a broad-brush question, but the answer can be relayed in three basic principles or skills.

There is a method to the madness. Yes, home stagers can visually create a room from scratch, but as they're trying to figure out where the couch goes and what should be placed on the wall, design principles are guiding their decisions. These principles of *balance, rhythm, harmony, emphasis, proportion,* and *scale* will help you succeed at distinguishing your home from your competition. So, with that said, before I end this e-book I want to leave you with the three broad skills that I call the "Prosperous Preps." These unique skills will help you succeed in the sale of your home, and they encompass the six basic principles of design.

As a home stager, whether I'm staging or designing a home, it's important to remember the basics and figure out how to utilize the space provided. While workers gutted the first floor of our home after Superstorm Sandy, I knew I wanted to rebuild the house better. The original layout had no real architectural features. With the walls and floors ripped down to the studs, I figured now was as good a time as any to create focal interest in the entryway, living room, dining room, and kitchen. So I created a plan to add a sliding glass door, a gas fireplace, more storage, and built-in seating.

Entryway is brighter & added a built-in on right side of walk through. Mounted TV, tiled the wall, and added a gas fireplace. Got rid of wall on right and added cabinetry. On left side of picture, added the sliding door.

The custom add-ons to this home are not only positive features—they also create *distinction* that would set our home apart from neighboring homes if we were to sell. This is our first broad principle.

Prosperous Prep #1: Distinction

As a home seller, it's important to know how to distinguish yourself from other homes on the market. In the 10 Steps to FEEL AT HOME process, I told you how to create distinction by researching a potential buyer's lifestyle and ways to emphasize your home. But just because you now know which wall the couch should be on or how to remove clutter doesn't mean the room will magically look like those on a magazine cover. Experts in our industry have extensive training in staging, design, and decorating, but we all follow the same six design principles mentioned above: balance, rhythm, harmony, emphasis, proportion, and scale. By understanding these principles, you'll be able to put together socially acceptable rooms.

Have you ever been in a room where it just feels off, but you can't exactly put your finger on what's wrong? Well, what's wrong is the design is breaking one or more of these principles. So, in order to avoid distracting buyers, let's go over each of these design principles in more detail:

Balance. We talked about balance in step eight of the "FEEL AT HOME" process, Optimize Space, but let's recap. Balance creates a feeling of equilibrium. It's all about distributing the visual weight of objects equally throughout the room. To determine the visual weight of an object, look at the item and ask yourself does it look heavy or light? A glass table has less visual weight than a wood table. A leather couch appears heavier than one with fabric. An object can even appear heavier depending on how low it is to the ground. To make a room balanced you must have a mixture of light and heavyweight objects. Balance is produced not just through shape, but through the color, pattern, and texture of an object. There are three different ways to create balance in a space:

- *Symmetrical:* This type of balance can be best described by inspiring a mirror image with the objects. Traditional or formal spaces call for symmetrical balance where the space is evenly split into two sides that mirror each other. Here is an example of symmetrical balance in this formal living room in Great Neck, Long Island.

We used two side tables and table lamps on either side of the couch. We also added two pillows on the couch. So, if you cut a line down the middle of the couch, both sides have similar balance.

- *Asymmetrical:* This type of balance is a bit harder to achieve because it's more complex and interesting. The visual weight of lines, colors, form, and textures are balanced without exact duplication. Asymmetrical balance creates an informal look. Take a look at the examples in this photo below of a Park Avenue living room in Manhattan. We had to work with a large column, an architectural feature that couldn't be changed. Stylish Stagers decided to balance the column with a floor lamp and mirror on one side of the couch, while using a side table and table lamp on the other side, where the column was located. Balancing the couch on the other side was a chair and TV stand the same height as the couch.

Before picture with column. Asymmetrical balance in this home staging transformation.

After we staged the home, keeping balance in mind without necessarily using the same objects.

- *Radial:* The last way to create balance in a room is through a radial approach. Basically, this is achieved when you have a central focal point and other objects radiate around the center. An example of this can be found in this photo of a kitchenette, located inside a Syosset home on Long Island.

The glass kitchen table with four chairs around it creates a radial balance with similar shapes, textures, and colors in the room.

Remember, the balance of the room is formed by the visual weight of the objects in the room. Balance and visual weight are decided based on the size of the room. A big room can hold more weight. Color, shape, and even patterns can affect the visual weight of an object.

Color. Neutral colors can remove weight in a room, while dark or bright colors add visual weight. That's why stagers always suggest making a room neutral; we want the room to feel light and airy.

Shape. A round shape has more visual weight than a rectangle. Think in terms of skinny and fat. The fatter the object, the more visual weight it will have in the room.

Pattern. Bold patterns can add weight, so unless you have a large room, use smaller patterns or solid colors to keep the room light.

Rhythm. This design principle is about creating a pattern of repetition to unify the space. What do I mean by this? You can use a specific object, color, shape, height, or texture throughout the room. These repetitions are what help you direct the buyer's eyes across the room. By using varying heights of objects, you create flow. The buyer has no choice but to look where you direct their eye. This is the secret to getting a buyer to see what you want them to see versus the other way around.

As I mentioned, color is a great way to add rhythm in a room. When using color, there is a common rule of 70-20-10; 70 percent of the room should be the lightest color, 20 percent should be the accent color, and 10 percent should be a contrasting accent color. Neutral colors such as white, black, or tan don't count toward these percentages unless they're used in more than 10 percent of the design.

Here is an example of using the color rule in an Upper East Side bedroom in New York City.

In this bedroom, notice we used the color of the walls as the theme of the room to create a cohesive feeling, especially since the homeowner didn't want

NYC bedroom after staging.
We used color to create a
unified space in this room.
(P.S. This bed is made out of
two blow-up mattresses!)

to paint the room a neutral color. So, according to the rule then, 70 percent of the design was green, 20 percent was white, and 10 percent was gold. When staging your rooms, make sure to use your accent color at least three times in visual range of one another to consider it repetition. Otherwise it may lack visual appeal and disrupt the eye flow of the room.

Another important part about rhythm and flow has to do with the shape of the objects used in the room, especially the furniture being used. You want buyers to easily navigate through each room, so be mindful of how much space there is between the furniture pieces. Try to mix shapes too! Having a rectangular sofa, with rectangular side tables, and a rectangular coffee table can get boring and too repetitive for the eye to maintain focus. In this case, create interest with a round or oval coffee table, then use round shades on the lamps placed on the rectangular side tables.

Harmony. Harmony is defined as a consistent, orderly, or pleasing arrangement of parts; congruity. In order to create harmony in your space, all the elements must be carefully chosen and act together to create a unified message. This message usually reveals a sense of restfulness, so it's especially nice to use this design principle in master bedrooms. An example of a way for a room to become harmonious is to use just one color when decorating or use furniture that takes a cue from the home's architectural structure. In other words, you can't have contemporary furnishings in a log cabin; it's not aesthetically pleasing.

Emphasis. A room where every object gets equal importance will most certainly distract buyers, and they'll have no idea what to look at first. Remember, we talked about how we want to direct the buyer's eye within the room and emphasize the positive features, or focal points. This was discussed in step seven of the FEEL AT HOME process called Highlight Positive Features. You can emphasize an architectural feature or a piece of furniture that is important to that room's purpose. Look to emphasize features like fireplaces, large windows, or built-ins and furniture such as a couch or a bed. You want the focal point to draw the buyer's eyes into the room.

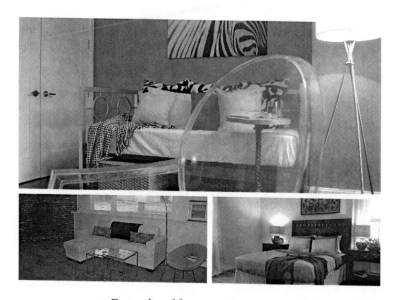

Examples of furniture focal points.
These homes were staged by Stylish Stagers Inc.

Proportion and Scale. Proportion relates to the ratio between the size of one part to another, while scale is how the size of one object relates to another or to the space in which it is placed. Each room or object is made up of parts that should be in proportion to one another for the room to be appealing. Start with the architectural features in the room. Are they proportionate to one another? Is each feature of similar size and weight? For example, do you have small windows on a large wall? While it's harder to change the proportions of architectural features in the room, furniture and decor also play a huge role in creating a proportionally designed room.

This design principle is one sellers commonly get wrong, especially when it comes to sizing up furnishings. We've all seen a small room with a large overstuffed sectional sofa or a dining room where you can barely squeeze by the chairs and the wall. Once you find the right size furniture to add to the space, pay close attention to the decor added. For instance, this dining room in Princeton, New Jersey, had one lonely small picture on the large focal wall. By changing out the picture with a larger one and flanking ironwork on either side to make it look even bigger, the wall decor is now in proportion and to scale with the rest of the objects in the room.

Dining room transformation after staging. Take a look at how adding larger wall decor now creates a harmonious proportional design that is pleasing to the eye.

In the before photo, the picture on the wall looks extremely small in comparison to everything else in the room. That's because the placement of different objects next to each other can exaggerate the size of one another. Scale has everything to do with relationship. Follow this simple formula when determining the scale of your room:

- What is the size of the room you're working with?
- Does your furniture match the size of the room? Think Goldilocks and the Three Bears: not too large, not too small, just right!
- Compare an object's visual weight, height, and size with each object throughout the room.

Remember, follow the six design principles—balance, rhythm, harmony, emphasis, proportion, and scale—to create a distinct look that will help you stand out among your competition on the real estate market. Look around your home to see if any of your rooms are breaking one or more of these design principles. Assess your windows, doors, fireplace, built-ins, furnishings, and decor. If something seems out of place, ask yourself does it have to do with the balance, rhythm, harmony, emphasis, proportion, or scale in the room? By understanding these principles and identifying what may be wrong with the room, you can then begin to fix the problem and compose a cohesive distinction in your home that buyers will fall in love with.

Are you having trouble identifying the potential problem? Let us help assess the problem; post a photo of the room on our Facebook fan page at www.facebook.com/homestagingtips.

Prosperous Prep #2: Service the Buyer

When a seller has their home on the market, it's important to appeal to buyers. That's why the second unique skill you need as a seller is knowing how to service the buyer. Once you decide to sell your home, it's time to shift your mindset from all about *you* to all about the *buyer*. Besides price, you've learned that a buyer usually makes a purchase based on emotional connection points, which home stagers like to tap into by using the five senses. When the buyer can see, smell, taste, hear, and feel the lifestyle of your home, they're more willing to consider purchasing your property. Here are a few ways home stagers use the five senses when preparing a property:

Sense of Sight. Within ten seconds of looking at a home, buyers have already made a decision based on their first impressions. Curb appeal that is warm and welcoming will ensure the buyers walk through the door, and this is determined through their sense of sight. Once inside, the other senses come into play. Let's explore.

Sense of Smell. We covered the issue of odors in detail earlier, so suffice it to say you want to keep your home clean and odor-free, infused with clean or fragrant scents. While pets are a big problem in this area, there are ways to keep buyers from detecting an animal in your home. As a proud owner of two dogs and two cats, I understand when homeowners are hesitant about removing their pets during the home-selling process. But when sellers overlook their pets, many times the real estate agent ends up with a snapshot of the furry little friends in the marketing pictures, rather than those magnificent built-ins, and that spells disaster when trying to attract buyers to the home online.

Before putting your pet-loving home on the market, get an honest assessment from a home stager or friend to determine what needs to be done to conceal the animals from potential buyers. Here are some products to help manage your pets during the selling process:

- Dogonit to help repair your grass from brown pee stains.
- Scoop Free Automatic Litter Box (it scoops away the contents and contains the smell for weeks at a time).
- Fresh Wave Odor Neutralizing Super Gel (safe for people and pets by using five essential oils to neutralize unwanted odor).
- Dyson DC25 Animal Vacuum (make sure to vacuum the furniture as well as carpet).
- FURminator (removes the pet's undercoat and can reduce shedding by 90 percent).

Like pet hair, it's important to maintain your animal's nails to avoid scratches on hardwood floors, carpet, or furniture. To avoid any more destruction to your home, while you're away give your pets rubbery toys that store treats. It should keep the pets entertained for hours rather than having them play with shoes, wood, or furniture.

While these products are a way for you to animal-proof your home when selling, you want to remove your animals during a showing or an open house. The animal's behavior, appearance, or cleanliness may distract buyers from opening their wallets. Not to mention leaving the animals behind gives your real estate agent automatic responsibility if something happens to your pet. What happens if the pet escapes while they're showing the home or, worse, attacks the buyer? So do yourself a favor and remove all pet items (leashes, cages, food bowls, toys, etc.), as well as your pet when a showing is scheduled.

Back to those marketing photos, it would be a shame to take all these steps but still have evidence of an animal living in your home from the online pictures. Over 93 percent of buyers start their home-buying search online, so make sure to cage or remove the animal(s) while photographing your home.

Sense of Taste. Look at buyers as guests in your home. Be a gracious host and offer drinks and snacks as a way to say thanks for stopping by. The lifestyle you're trying to portray will determine what to serve. For instance, if it's a luxury condo on the market offer a Bellini cocktail and crepes; if you're selling a country home offer lemonade and fruit (especially sliced watermelon.) Use tastes to jog a buyer's childhood memories to help them relate to the home.

Sense of Hearing. Sounds can be a positive or negative energy in a home. If a property is beachside, leaving the windows open to hear the ocean waves and seagulls will remind buyers why they're looking to live at the beach. In contrast, if a home is near a major highway it's important to drown out the noise. You can use a water fountain or soothing music to reduce the negative noise.

Sense of Touch. Buyers like to touch things, so make sure doorknobs, pulleys, banisters, and furniture are all clean. Buyers will open cabinets, sit on furniture, and touch anything they can get their hands on. To promote this sense, add different textures throughout the home such as using soft throws and pillows to accentuate the coziness of the space.

The ultimate goal is to keep potential buyers in the space as long as possible. If buyers feel comfortable in the home, they will stay longer. Using the five senses to promote a home is an easy way to guide a buyer to make an offer.

Prosperous Prep #3: Excellence

The first two unique skills needed to obtain success when selling your home, *distinction* and *service the buyer*, are nothing without excellence. This third unique skill will help you put everything you learned about home staging into perspective. Now, I'm not saying your home needs to be perfect. There is no such thing as perfect, but I would like you to strive for excellence. The word *excellent* means to possess outstanding quality, and isn't that what you want to promote to buyers, that your home is the best there is on the market?

Too often, though, I find that a seller's perception of excellence becomes unknowingly compromised by certain circumstances and rationalizations that have seeped into the way they measure their performance. Without knowing it, your habits and attitudes can affect your excellence at home, at work, and in life.

Let's take selling your home, for example. I recently worked with a client, Laurie P., who was sick of her house. She complained about the space and the layout. She stopped cleaning because she just didn't care about the appearance of her space. She didn't see the value in her home anymore despite asking for over-market value.

If you as a seller don't think of your home as a prized possession, how can you give the buyer your best? It's impossible! The problem was that's not how Laurie felt about her home when she moved in, or else why did she buy it? I needed her to tap into those initial feelings she had about her home to get motivated about the staging upkeep and get her home sold. It was a challenge to get her to strive for excellence toward something she had already written off, but then I taught her about the law of excellence I learned from the book *Who Kidnapped Excellence? What Stops Us from Giving and Being Our Best* by Harry Paul, John Britt, and Ed Jent.

In this book the authors zero in on five core qualities of excellence that are needed to provide outstanding quality. As a seller, since you're trying to obtain excellence in showing your home, it seems fitting to explain how your passion, competency, flexibility, communication, and ownership can affect the sale of your home.

Passion. Most people try to start their day off right, but then somehow the daily grind may get to them. With passion, you get to choose your attitude, so why not choose the best one? See life as an opportunity and be willing to go the extra mile. Laurie saw her home as routine, ordinary, and blinded herself to the flaws of her home because she no longer wanted to deal with them. She wasn't looking at her home with fresh eyes, which was hurting the sale of her home.

The authors in the book explain, "Develop a habit of approaching each day with a great attitude. Whatever door you need to go through, do it like it's the first time you've ever been through that door, like you can't wait to go out and explore," much like a dog does when let outside. Yes, the dog goes out the same door several times a day, but each time the dog is excited, trembling with anticipation, and can't wait to get out there and explore.

After rearranging Laurie's home and organizing her closets, she looked at her home in a new way. By shaking up her routine, the transformation made her passionate about maintaining the space, which kept the home in better condition for showings.

Competency. Knowledge is power and gives you the ability to sell your home not just successfully but efficiently. As a reader of this e-book, you're demonstrating your competency by challenging yourself to learn home staging techniques that will benefit your bottom line. You're learning what, when, and how to stage your home.

The authors of *Who Kidnapped Excellence?* write, "If you can develop a way of seeing the 'next person in the process' as your customer, then you can give them your best. When you approach them from that perspective, communication begins to flow." Laurie worked in customer service and valued her customers. When I asked her to view a homebuyer as a customer, she actually began asking her real estate agent for feedback; she wanted to know what she could do better for the next buyer. By empowering herself with knowledge of what her buyer wanted, she was able to easily accept the changes being made in her home, and Laurie quickly sold her home because of her competency.

Flexibility. As Laurie accepted change, she became more flexible for buyers. During the first few weeks when her home was on the market prior to staging, she had a strict schedule and only allowed the real estate agent to show her home on a certain day at a certain time. Unfortunately, when you're selling your home, your needs and privacy go out the window. It's important to respond to unique situations with buyers and accommodate their needs whenever possible. With flexibility, you must be willing to accept new ideas and methods without compromising your values.

Eventually Laurie became more lenient with showings, which made her more flexible when it came to negotiating the sale of her home. There was a termite issue with her home that was obviously out of her control, but could have jeopardized the deal. Laurie's flexibility in solving the problem got her one step closer to the closing table.

Communication. Look around your home. What is currently being communicated to a potential buyer? In Laurie's case, prior to staging, her home said small, neglected, and no storage space to buyers, among other negative interactions. Although Laurie didn't physically speak these words, they were being nonverbally communicated to buyers. Can you really afford any subliminal confusion? With communication, it's important to listen intently and speak with clarity.

With staging, you have to dictate the nonverbal communication being made between you and the buyer; the message can then be received the way you intended it. Remember, even if you're not saying anything, your actions could be speaking volumes.

Ownership. Rather than writing off your house as Laurie did in the beginning of the sales process, own your home. Think back to when you unlocked the door to your new home. How did you feel? Most likely you were a proud owner and couldn't wait to show off your new lifestyle to family and friends. Now is the time to use those feelings to get the next homeowners excited about home ownership. Take charge of your actions, behavior, and performance while your home is on the market.

The law of excellence is described in the book as keeping a constant awareness and vigilance of these five core qualities: passion, competency, flexibility, communication, and ownership. Most of us want to be the best at what we do and who we are, so don't let average quietly creep in and kidnap your excellence, or it could prohibit a deal from happening. By striving for excellence when preparing and showcasing your home for sale, you're putting your best foot forward, which will be reflected in the final dollar amount, reassuring you that no money was left behind on the closing table.

In fact, these "Prosperous Preps" of *distinction, service the buyer,* and *excellence* are skills you can use throughout the course of your life again and again at work, at home, or personally to gain success.

Chapter 8

TRUSTING YOUR ACT

We've come a long way. If I've successfully fulfilled the FEEL AT HOME mission, then I hope you are now inspired and instructed on how to improve your home. You can make a difference and more money with what you now know when preparing your home for sale. You now understand the benefit of home staging and realize that it's more valuable than you ever imagined. You can quickly improve your chances on the market if you simply position, package, promote, and partner with a real estate team to get your home sold.

You can do this. Now is your time. There's potential in your home to create a lifestyle buyers will aspire to so you can get the best return on your investment. Even if it takes longer than a few hours or days to sell your home, you're choosing to be proactive, and the right buyer will notice all your hard work. There is a meaningful satisfaction in knowing you've helped someone achieve the American dream of owning a home, which represents freedom and independence.

If you've read this far, then you know more about home staging than the average seller and can leverage that to beat out your competition. I'm excited to hear what you do with this newfound knowledge. You have a great foundation and a huge head start when it comes to selling your home, because few people know how to utilize home staging. If you run into a homeowner selling their home, please give them this e-book or tell them to visit www.toritoth.com so I can help them get on the fast track toward the closing table.

I don't know why you're reading my words, but I feel honored that our paths have crossed and that I've been able to share with you what I've learned on my journey to FEEL AT HOME. I'm still learning. Home stagers are always learning new techniques and trends to help sellers. After working on hundreds of houses, I do have one strong assumption about why you have landed on this page and found my message at this point in your life. I believe you're here because deep within you know it's time to move on. Perhaps you've stumbled onto a life event out of your control, such as job loss, death, or divorce. Or perhaps it's time to evaluate your space because of a new baby, or because your kids are all grown. Regardless, I believe your being here has something profound to do with your lifestyle—stepping into the second act of your show, to FEEL AT HOME once again.

While it may be scary for you to move on to your second act, prolonging the inevitable, playing with the real estate market, or neglecting your home won't prevent life from happening around you. I realized that as I watched my neighbors continue to struggle with repairing their homes a year after Superstorm Sandy and when I see potential clients refusing to merchandise their property properly, choosing to go on the market as-is instead.

To "feel at home" is to belong or feel accepted. Without following the ten-step process, you may find yourself on the market with no buyer interest. It certainly doesn't make anyone feel accepted when no one cares about what you're selling. This is your time to sell. Work through the material found in this e-book. Start now by taking one room of your home at a time and going through the ten-step process. Figure out the first impressions being made in each room, determine who will be buying your home and what they like, then decide what will stay and what can go. Be sure to make those necessary repairs and improvements before putting each room back together again with furniture and accessories that will appeal to the buyer.

Be open to change and obtain that seller's mindset which can alter bad habits and help you strive for excellence. You may find some days to be a challenge; you'll be too tired to do the dishes, declutter the closet, or deal with the painter, but that's when these lessons will come in handy. Remember nothing is permanent, and the faster you implement home staging into your home, the faster you'll move on from the constant cleaning, decluttering, and foot traffic through your personal space. Trust that once your home is staged, you'll get interested buyers to see your act and find that one who feels right at home, willing to give you the standing ovation you've asked for and deserve.

Happy selling!

—Tori

ACKNOWLEDGMENTS

It's been a pleasure writing this e-book that has been on my to-do list for some time now. I hope you find it to be a wealth of knowledge you can use not only in the sale of your home, but in other areas of your life. This e-book took some time to research and create in a logical way for homeowners to understand and utilize.

That's why I dedicate this e-book to my husband, Sal Arena. His patience, understanding, and belief in me continue to push me to accomplish my goals. Without him, I don't know how my life would be, and for that I'll be forever grateful.

To my home staging mentors, Audra Slinkey, Matthew Finlason, Melissa Marro, Lisa McIntee, Karen Otto, and Shell Brodnax, who taught me everything I know about this industry. They helped distinguish my home staging techniques and have been just a call, email, or plane ride away whenever I find myself in need of advice.

My completion of this e-book could not have been accomplished without the guidance of Brendon Burchard, bestselling author and founder of Experts Academy and Total Product Blueprint. Thank you for inspiring me to share my message.

Finally, to all my past and future clients, I am honored to be able to help you move on to your second act. This is an industry for which many still don't quite understand the value, but you did! You gave me a chance, and for that many heartfelt thanks.

ABOUT THE AUTHOR

Tori Toth has been blessed to feel at home again in her Howard Beach bungalow after surviving Superstorm Sandy in 2012. Since then, she has dedicated her life to helping homeowners, builders, investors, and realtors create a lifestyle homebuyers will aspire to. As a professional home staging expert, trained through Home Staging Resource and by HGTV star Matthew Finlason of *The Stagers*, she has prepared hundreds of clients' homes focusing on target staging and lifestyle merchandising.

It has always been Tori's initiative to educate home sellers on ways to prepare and showcase their homes for sale. That's why she is not only an active member of the Real Estate Staging Association (RESA), but she's created a series of "how-to" home staging videos that have been watched over 100,000 times on YouTube and have helped her reach home sellers near and far. Tori's goal is "to make home staging a real estate standard." She has been interviewed by CNN Money and *Long Island Weekly* and is a contributor for *Mann Report Residential*.

Tori donates a portion of the proceeds from *Feel At Home* to All Hands Volunteers and Habitat for Humanity. She lives in New York City with her husband and her four fur babies. To meet her or learn how to work with Tori, please visit www.toritoth.com.

CPSIA information can be obtained at www.ICGtesting.com
Printed in the USA
LVOW11s1812120716

496014LV00007B/968/P